WHEN
the Wave Comes,
TAKE YOUR TIME

Melanie Michelle Rosenthal

Copyrights © 2025

All Rights Reserved

No part of this book may be reproduced or transmitted in any form or by any means, electronic or mechanical, including photocopying, recording, or by any information storage and retrieval system without the written permission of the author, except where permitted by law.

For my beloved girls,

Mariella Leilani and Emilie Lanea,

my inspiration.

In memory of the victims of Lahaina 2023.

ACKNOWLEDGMENTS

I would like to thank my husband, Dirk, for his constant patience and for always supporting me with my ideas and wishes.

You can't stop the waves, but you can learn to surf.

JON KABAT-ZINN

TABLE OF CONTENTS

Foreword 11
July 2023 13
The Arrival 39
The Surf School 54
Culture Hawaii 76
School 81
Ocean Sisters 99
Lahaina 107
Storm 120
Hawaii Lei Wedding 137
Surfing Competition 165
Kauai 199
Invitation 222
In Flames 241
The Legacy 265
About the Author 272

FOREWORD

ALOHA

In February 2017, I was gently carried through the water by waves on a surfboard for the first time on the coast of Maspalomas. This experience is one of my happiest moments. It captivated me so much that I've been trying to surf at Atlantic dream spots ever since, as often as possible. When my sweet girls, Mariella and Emilie, were old enough, I taught them to surf. I love sitting in the lineup with them and waiting for the waves to roll in. It's the spot in the surf where the waves form perfectly for surfers to pop up and rush down into the wave's hollow. I wanted to share the experience with my girls, and that is how my story was born. I want to encourage you to book a surf lesson so you can experience for yourself what I'm talking about. It is pure freedom. I chose Maui because it's a small, beautiful

Hawaiian island in the middle of the Pacific. What's crazy is that I have a family there, but I haven't met them yet. The reason for this is quite simple. I don't want to meet my Hawaiian father, who left me and my siblings at a young age. So, I'll tell you about my dream, the beauty of the island of Maui, our passion for surfing, and how I imagine meeting my unknown family in Hawaii.

Mahalo,

I am waiting for you.

LINE UP!

JULY 2023

"Why do we have to move abroad?" Lanea asked her older sister, Leilani.

Lanea's name was of Hawaiian origin and meant 'the heavenly one.' At nine years old, she was very physically fit. She wore her wild blonde hair at medium length. Her almond-shaped, large green eyes shone out of her pointed oval face. With her dimples and full lips, she looked a lot like her father, Dirk. She loved playing soccer and doing gymnastics. In short, she was a helpful, energetic girl with lots of imagination.

Leilani, her 15-month older sister—translated into Hawaiian as "the child of heaven"—was also athletically built and only a little taller. Her straight mahogany-brown hair was also medium-length. Her large eyes were bright brown. She had inherited them from her mother, Melanie. Leilani was always friendly to her friends. She gave comfort when it was needed.

Her hobbies were drawing and gymnastics. She was open-hearted, sensitive, and funny.

But as different as the girls were in character or appearance, they had one thing in common: Water was both of their element.

Leilani was cuddled up next to her younger sister on an old mattress on the floor. The midsummer promised only mild temperatures and lots of rain. It was to be the family's last night in western Germany for the time being.

Leilani comforted her younger sister with the words: "Because it's mom's dream! Here in Germany, winter is always cold and long. The economy is going down the drain, and the healthcare system is now crumbling, too."

"You got that from Dad!" Lanea laughed at her.

Leilani nodded and winked at her. Lanea couldn't react quickly enough to her kiss attack, so she endured it and then washed the spit off her cheek, slightly disgusted.

Leilani laughed back loudly and whispered, "Let's wait and see. Hawaii will be exciting, and we can go out to sea and surf all day."

"I'm really looking forward to that!"

"I hope Mom and Dad keep their promise. If we're unhappy there, we'll move back!"

"Our house will remain unsold for 365 days," Leilani promised her sister.

"Let's go to sleep; a long day awaits us!" Leilani murmured in her direction.

They snuggled closer together and fell asleep.

The next morning, they were woken up early by their mom, Melanie, with a good-humored ALOHA.

Melanie was in her late 30s, athletic, of medium height, and looked very much like her daughter, Leilani. Her dark complexion and her dark, thick, curly hair suggested that she was of Hawaiian origin. She looked like one of those girls in Hawaii who would dance the hula in bamboo skirts.

Melanie's father was a native Hawaiian and a US soldier who was transferred to Germany for his job. He met Melanie's mother there, who fell head over heels and blindly followed him to Texas. He left the family when Melanie was still young and they never had contact with him again.

The house in North Rhine-Westphalia that they lived in for 23 years was in a remote location in an industrial area. It was white brick and about 300 square meters in size. With a small garden and a large heated pool, they had a great time there as a family and with their friends. Leilani and Lanea learned to swim very early on. They loved the water. In summer, it felt like they spent from morning to night in it. They were always diving and splashing around.

Their father, Dirk, was waiting downstairs and called up the stairs, "Children, we have to go soon!"

Dirk was a little older than Melanie. She liked his brown doe eyes and short blond hair, especially when his skin was a little tanned from the short summer. He was tall and athletically built. They fell in love when Melanie completed her apprenticeship as an industrial clerk at his company.

For 20 years, he worked as a junior manager in his parents' company. When his parents died, first his father and then his mother, he became the successor to the company that his parents had built up. It was a medium-sized company that manufactured and processed security systems. His father was a mechanical engineer and had designed and built great machines from which his parents were able to make a good living.

Now, Dirk had to make a painful decision. After all, how was he supposed to look after his company if he soon wanted to live in the middle of the Pacific? With a heavy heart, he had his share paid out by his siblings.

Melanie also ran a successful small business in the care sector. Her employees were very important to her and very close to her heart. But even she could no longer look after them. She, therefore, sold her business to her best friend, Janna, who had run the care facility with her for years.

"Have our things arrived at our house on Maui yet?" Lanea asked her parents at breakfast, looking a little sadly into the empty living room.

"Our furniture and belongings were already set up as planned by the moving company in our house in Maui a week ago!" Melanie said encouragingly.

"Let's go, kids! Franky is here, and he's driving us to the airport," Dirk announced happily.

Franky was the sales manager of his company. He was also Melanie and Dirk's best man. He was not only the best salesman in their eyes but also a highly talented craftsman. At 1.80 meters tall, with his curly gray hair and his good and cheerful mood, the family had grown very fond of him.

Everyone was very quiet on the journey, with only Franky providing an atmospheric narration.

"I'm jealous. I want to come, too. Will you take me with you?"

Leilani and Lanea laughed. He was always good for jokes.

Before Leilani and Lanea were born, Melanie and Dirk often visited the Hawaiian Islands.

"I don't have it as good as you guys," Franky emphasized.

And again, the whole family laughed; he was also good at cheering up others.

"I wasn't born in America, so I have to stay here," said Franky.

Melanie was aware that she had a family in Hawaii. As she wanted no contact with her father, it was difficult to find relatives. Perhaps once she had settled in Hawaii, she would certainly start looking for relatives. But that wasn't important right now. She leaned back and thought about the time when her parents had moved back to Germany from El Paso, Texas. At first, they lived in an ugly apartment block. Her mother worked as a housekeeper for a rich family, while her father worked as a machine operator in an old wire drawing mill. The two of them often argued and somehow never got along. One day, her father decided to take the whole family to Hawaii. But her mother didn't want to be separated from her family again. She simply suffered too much from being homesick. The decision made him spiteful for a long time. Melanie hardly recognized him anymore. One day, he was simply gone.

At the airport in Frankfurt, they said goodbye to Franky, made their way through security, and waited for their flight to be called at their gate.

Leilani was sitting on a bench. Her sad look revealed that she was thinking of her family and friends. Her bright eyes became cloudy until sweet tears rolled unstoppably down her slightly reddened cheeks.

As Lanea looked into her face, she felt sorry for her and fought against her sister's emotions. But she didn't succeed for long, and soon, tears began to roll down from her green almond eyes. The other passengers noticed her sobs and expectantly looked at Melanie and Dirk. Only then did they realize what was happening to their girls. When Melanie looked at them, she trembled.

She was overcome with shame and briefly felt her spirit leave her body. Self-doubt and nausea were overwhelming her. How could she ask her two sweet girls to leave their friends, their sport, and their family? To simply drag them off to a foreign country with a different language. Her spirit returned because she had to stay strong, and so she comforted her girls with the following words: "All dreams can come true if we have the courage to follow them."

After a while, the girls felt a little better. Their parents cheered the girls up with a little snack from their favorite bakery. They were crazy about those wheat rolls with ham and cheese.

Their flight was now called up, and experience had shown that older and disabled people, as well as families with children, were called first for check-in. Melanie and Dirk knew that Lanea and Leilani were no longer toddlers, but the flight attendants hadn't said anything to them yet. So off they went. It was a Boeing 767 with

259 seats. Dirk wanted his family to have a comfortable journey, so he had booked Economy Plus seats, which allowed more legroom than Economy.

"Mom, which seat numbers do we have?" the girls asked excitedly as they waited on the passenger bridge to board the plane.

"Rows 22 and 23, seats A and B," Dirk answered them and looked at the flight tickets with narrowed eyes. He had been wearing reading glasses for some time, but they were in his backpack.

"We'll take row 22," the girls called out at the same time. Two young, blonde flight attendants in blue uniforms smiled and greeted the family with a friendly "Hello" and went to meet them.

Dirk had always been a little afraid of flying. As soon as he boarded the plane, he listened to the sound of the air conditioning. He noticed the airflow from the fresh air vents.

The family was totally impressed by the seats. Of course, the seats in first class were more comfortable, but nobody was unhappy. The children took their entertainment equipment, such as coloring materials and iPads, out of their backpacks and made themselves comfortable.

When all the passengers were on board and their hand luggage was stowed above their heads, Dirk listened to the click of each seatbelt. The doors were closed, and the emergency slides were activated.

They seemed to be on their way. Melanie was amazed at how punctually they were taking off and looked at her watch.

"As planned, 12:15," she remarked.

Leilani and Lanea took the menu card and the duty-free catalog out of their seat bags and studied them. The safety instructions were announced. Melanie and Dirk watched attentively as the pretty flight attendant imitated the safety instructions.

The purser, i.e., the cabin manager, instructed them through the speakers. Melanie looked around and was annoyed by the passengers who had already prepared to sleep.

The flight attendants stood in the aisles and tried to explain how to put on oxygen masks correctly and how to put on life jackets in an emergency while the dozing passengers, with their eyes closed and headphones in their ears, were already getting really comfortable on their seats sitting down. She and Dirk secretly hoped that there would never be a situation in which they would need the oxygen masks and life jackets.

The plane began to move, and the captain spoke through the speakers, "Ladies and gentlemen, dear children, welcome on board. Our flight will take eleven hours. We would, therefore, ask you to follow our safety instructions. Our crew is always available to answer your questions. Should we expect turbulence, we will inform you in good time. We wish you a pleasant flight."

"We're moving!" shouted a little boy, one row in front of the girls. He stood up in his seat and tried to make contact with the girls. They smiled at him. Ashamed, he quickly turned around and sat down.

Dirk had once seen a documentary about air trust. "The engines aren't running yet," he pondered.

He noticed that the sound of the air conditioning had stopped. Not much air was flowing through the fresh air nozzles either. This was because compressed air from the auxiliary power unit was needed to start the engines.

He heard the humming of an engine, first the right one, then the left one. The light in the cabins flickered a little; now he knew that the power supply had been switched.

It was no longer the auxiliary power unit in the rear but the large engines that produced enough power for all the systems on board via a generator. The plane rocked a little and rolled over the joints in the apron concrete.

Meanwhile, Melanie leaned over to her girls. "Are you all right? Are you excited?

The light went out, and she could just hear them say, "Yes, Mom." The engines howled, and a small jolt went through the plane.

Melanie looked at Dirk and gently stroked his shoulder. "Airplanes are built to fly," she whispered to him. She knew that would calm him down a little.

A fraction of a second later, they were pressed into their seats, and immediately after take-off, the landing gear was retracted. They were in the air now. Melanie saw how her husband was suffering. She also thought that the take-off and landing were always the most exciting. Now, she made herself comfortable and studied the magazines she had bought at the airport.

When Dirk felt confident and relaxed, he took his laptop out of his backpack and watched a movie he had uploaded the night before. This relaxed him and distracted him from his fear of flying. Melanie read a report about e-foil surfboards in her surf magazine.

This has nothing to do with real surfing anymore, she thought, a little irritated, and closed the magazine. A friendly flight attendant asked her if she needed anything. But Melanie kindly waved her off.

She leaned back, closed her eyes and thought about the time when her family had no idea how great her desire was to one day live by the sea. She remembered that moment when she was gently carried through the water by waves and became obsessed with surfing.

In 2017, Melanie had booked an all-inclusive vacation on Gran Canaria for her and her family. Leilani was just three years old, and Lanea was only two, and they needed all their attention. When Melanie and Dirk took their girls to the beach in the south of the island, Melanie looked enviously at all the surfers sitting on their surfboards in the water or surfing. Dirk could see from her bright brown eyes that she wanted to try it, too. But she hesitated for a few days because she didn't want to leave him alone with their two little girls while she enjoyed herself at sea. It was exhausting looking after two bundles of energy. The vacation was due to end soon, so Melanie decided to find a surf school after all. Her desire to surf outweighed her willingness to help.

He'll be fine for a few hours, she decided. So she watched the surfers disappearing with their surfboards along the beach promenade between restaurants without a trace. She wondered and thought, *There can't be a surf school there, can there?* She watched for a while as surfers with or without surfboards in wetsuits emerged from a cellar while she played in the sand with her girls.

"Honey! Just go down there," she heard Dirk say, a little annoyed.

She set off with a tingling sensation in her stomach. She really wanted to learn how to surf. She slowly walked down the steep basement stairs and stood in a large room with white tiles.

A poster with a large wave printed on it hung on the wall to the right. Next to it was a small palm tree. Straight ahead, surfboards in different colors leaned against the wall. Clothes racks with wetsuits hanging from them were lined up in the left-hand corner. In front of them, she saw two self-made changing rooms with hibiscus curtains. She liked the decor of the surf school. It was lovingly decorated with artificial flower leis. Suddenly, a man stepped in front of her and greeted her.

"ALOHA!" she heard a male voice say.

"Aloha here in Spain?" she said quietly. But she liked it. It fit with the decor of the surf school. She hadn't seen him approach her. He was about 40 years old, tanned, dark-haired, out rageously muscular; he could only be Spanish. A dainty blonde beauty stepped up next to him and asked if she could help her. Melanie started small talk with them and got an appointment for 9 am the next morning. They were both very friendly. They lived the aloha spirit through and through. The Canary Islands were perfect for this because of the climate. She happily jumped up the cellar stairs to the beach and told Dirk about the appointment. She really just wanted the day to pass quickly. Melanie was really looking forward to the next morning and went to bed early. Totally excited and happy, she fell asleep.

After breakfast, Melanie went to the beach alone, as Dirk wanted to head down later with the girls in a relaxed manner.

She walked down the beach promenade as quickly as possible. When she reached the cellar, slightly out of breath, she came across five surfers in wetsuits.

"Am I too late?" she asked the Spanish surf instructor.

"ALOHA! The others are too early." He grinned at her. His manner was so relaxed that he seemed content and balanced.

He looked her over briefly and gave her a wetsuit changing room. The curtain, left or right, couldn't be closed completely. It was sewn a little too narrow. She decided to close the curtain on the right-hand side. This meant that the changing room was a little open, but most of the action took place to her right.

Getting into a wetsuit quickly was a great skill for her at that moment. She sat there in the changing room and didn't know what to do. She did not want to call anyone for help. But the wetsuit was clinging to her knees.

"It has to work somehow," she said quietly but was completely annoyed. The more the time passed, the harder she pulled on the thing like in a fury until she had won the battle with the wetsuit and stepped out of the changing room drenched in sweat. She joined the group with an affected smile on her face. The surf instructor handed everyone a surfboard and a long cable.

Melanie was surprised because her surfboard was bigger than the one the other classmates had been given.

"Why am I getting such a huge surfboard?" she asked the surf instructor.

"You're a beginner; the bigger the surfboard, the more fun you'll have out there."

A little disappointed, she trusted the surf instructor's statement. She dragged the huge, heavy surfboard and cable out of the cellar and a few more meters along the beach.

"How exhausting," she said to the others. She hadn't exhausted. The sun was shining brightly in the sky and warming the still-empty beach. The beach was huge and surrounded by large sand dunes. They laid the surfboards in a row on the warm white sand. First, the surf instructor explained how to attach the cable to the surfboard. Then, he strapped the other end of the cable around his left ankle. Melanie quickly realized that it was a leash. A leash established the connection between the surfboard and the surfer. Joy welled up inside her.

The surf instructor showed them dry runs, which the surf students had to imitate. He showed them the correct position to lay down on the surfboard.

"Not too high, then you'll fall into the wave; not too low, then the wave will roll away without you," he warned them. He taught them to keep their bodies tense. "Paddle with long, fast strokes and jump onto the surfboard as quickly as possible. Try to keep your arms still; otherwise, you'll lose your balance."

Melanie lay on her huge surfboard and repeated the exercises until sweat dripped from her forehead. The sun also played its part.

"How am I supposed to remember all this? The wave breaks within seconds," she said to the group.

But no one answered. Her courage was failing her. She felt like running away.

The surf instructor clapped his hands loudly and said, "Here we go. Into the water. We have great waves."

Melanie looked out to sea and took a closer look at the waves. The waves were around 1.3 meters high and rolled in relatively quickly, one after the other. She grabbed her surfboard and ran into the water after the others. Despite the neoprene shoes, the water seemed terribly cold to her. It was just February, but the desire to surf trumped the icy feeling. She fought her way through a few waves on the surfboard, which quickly warmed her up. She no longer felt the cold.

The things a wetsuit could do. It had to be good for something. The surf instructor held the surfboard by the back. Melanie lay down on it and slid back and forth until she was in the right position. She watched as the others rushed past her. She wanted to do that, too. She heard the surf instructor call out, "Paddle!"

So she started paddling.

"Faster," he shouted. And she paddled faster. She felt a jolt and fell over the front into the breaking wave. The wave pushed her underwater for a few seconds. Melanie was completely at its mercy. As the wave rolled on, Melanie was able to surface again. She pulled the surfboard back toward her by the leash.

Completely confused, she looked around. Her hair was cold and soaking wet on her head. The surf instructor gave her a "thumbs up" when she caught sight of him between the glittering waves. He made sure she was alright.

Puzzled, she also gave him the all-clear with a "thumbs up." She was amazed that she had survived. Over-motivated, she paddled off enthusiastically. She tried again and again. Either she fell off the surfboard again, or she didn't get the wave.

Maybe it's the huge surfboard, she thought briefly.

The surf instructor always gave her good tips. "Keep your arms still; try to get up faster," she heard him say again and again.

Tired, she looked toward the beach and suddenly saw her cute girls standing there. They waved to her and were happy to see her. Dirk held them tight; otherwise, they would have just run into the water. She lay there on her surfboard, and the waves rolled underneath her. She had to manage to stay standing for once.

Body tension, upper body, paddle hard, jump up, and keep your arms steady, she thought. The surf instructor held her surfboard again. She nodded resolutely at him. Melanie paddled off hard, as he pushed her forward slightly, and she stood up and stayed standing for the first time. She held her arms in the usual calm surfing position. Now, for the first time, she was gently carried through the water to her girls' feet by the most incredible wave. Overwhelmed by this feeling, she jumped off the surfboard and showered her girls with lots of kisses. She looked back out to sea, where the rest of the group gave her a joyful hang-loose salute. She knew the sign and greeted them back. The "hang-loose" greeting had established itself among surfers worldwide. In Hawaii, the gesture was everywhere and an integral part of the local culture. She took a break and sat down on her surfboard. She was overwhelmed by the feeling; it was pure freedom. The girls saw the surfboard as a kind of toy and jumped around on it, beaming with joy.

Melanie discovered her passion for surfing that day. She decided to run a surf school herself one day and live by the sea.

She returned from her memories when a flight attendant came to serve them a hot meal.

After a very pleasant and quiet flight, they landed at San Francisco International Airport eleven hours later. The flight to Maui was scheduled for two hours later. It was 2:15 p.m. local time. The family looked for their next gate, which was on the other side of the airport. Tired but happy to have survived the first flight in good health, they walked through the huge airport, past several stores and restaurants to their new gate and waited together for the airline that would take them to the Valley Isle. They had a great view of their plane from the huge airport windows. The plane was much smaller this time. A Boeing 717-200 with 110 seats. The girls particularly liked the print on the plane. It was a white plane with a pretty woman's face printed on the fuselage. The orange plumeria she wore in her hair was striking. The airline's rudders were painted pink and purple. Below her, a silver maile lei with woven Pakalana flowers wound its way up to the fuselage of the plane.

"Mom, is it a certain woman?" asked Leilani. She looked at Melanie expectantly and hoped she would be able to give her a suitable answer.

"I remember reading about her. I can't remember her name. But I do know that she was Miss Hawaii in 1964."

"You're so great, Mom." Leilani looked at her mom honestly.

Melanie smiled and winked at her. Lanea was incredibly good at giving compliments. The call of airline HI203 boomed through the loudspeakers, and the family went off first, as they always did, with the other passengers following them in their summer outfits.

Dirk had booked Economy Plus seats for the family, even though the flight was only scheduled to last 5.5 hours. They were seated in rows 10 and 11, seats A and B. Leilani and Lanea played around on the screens. Integrated screens on short-haul flights were rare. By now, the two of them knew their way around airplanes and their equipment. The family had traveled as often as possible in recent years. It was important to Melanie and Dirk to show them as much of the world as they could.

In Germany, it was already 2 in the morning, but in San Francisco, it was just 4:15 in the afternoon. The fact that there were several time zones in between meant that the family's natural time system was altered, and they were getting more tired by the hour. The pilot greeted his passengers with words of encouragement.

The plane took off, and Dirk was relieved when the seatbelt lights above his head went out. He watched another movie to distract himself. Melanie spent the last two hours of the flight in a trance. She fell asleep, woke up again and again, and felt dizzy with fatigue. The plane rattled constantly. Bright lights flashed through the plane windows.

The seatbelt signs lit up.

Dirk looks scared, Melanie thought to herself as she woke up briefly. Her tiredness meant that she was in no way able to help him.

The girls slept soundly, and their heads rolled back and forth over their neck pillows. The plane shook enormously. They had never experienced turbulence like this before.

A young woman from Texas was chattering away at Melanie in her American English. She talked like a waterfall. Melanie wanted to have a conversation with her, but she found it difficult. She only understood half of what she was saying because she was talking way too fast. When the young woman realized that she wasn't answering her, she left Melanie alone. She was finally able to get some sleep, like the rest of the family.

As she slept, she had a bad dream. She was on a plantation in Hawaii; it was hot, and the sky was bright blue. The wonderful smell of coffee filled the air. She was holding a coffee bean in her hand when Dirk suddenly pulled on her. People started screaming and running. The volcano that was directly in front of them suddenly collapsed. Hot clouds of embers and ash flowed down the slope at great speed, taking everything with them. The sky went black, and then she woke up.

Dirk looked at her. "Are you all right?" he asked her worriedly.

She gave him a friendly nod and kept her nightmare to herself. She looked at her watch, but she could no longer tell anything from it. She had lost track of time.

She calculated back and forth. The pilot announced through the loudspeakers that they would be landing in 20 minutes. Melanie and Dirk were very grateful for this news.

"Please fold the tables and put your seat backs forward," said the flight attendant.

Melanie looked at her sweet sleeping girls. With their mouths open, they had fallen into a deep sleep. She quietly folded their tables forward and gently woke them with a kiss on their foreheads. Sleepy and disoriented, they both rubbed their eyes.

"We'll be there soon! I can't wait to see what Hawaii has in store for us," Melanie whispered to them. The children rolled their eyes. Their hair was matted from the constant tossing and turning. They looked like cute flodders. But Melanie didn't mind. There was no point nagging them after such a long journey. She probably looked really worn out herself. She turned on her camera and looked at her reflection in it.

I'll be fine, a bit of sleep, and then I'll be my old self again, she thought.

The plane landed incredibly softly. They were preparing to set foot in another world in the middle of the Pacific, hopefully with lots of adventures, plenty of sunshine, and lots of ALOHA.

THE ARRIVAL

19 hours later, they landed at Kahului airport. The family was exhausted from the long journey. They left the passenger bridge and ran after the other passengers to the baggage claim area. Warm air flowed through the corridors of the airport. The girls trotted after their parents.

"It feels like a vacation," Lanea said to her sister, Leilani.

"Only this time it's not," emphasised Leilani. Large advertising posters hung on the walls of the airport. Posters advertising scuba diving, surfing, the North Shore—one of the world's most famous venues for surfing competitions—whale watching, the Road to Hana—one of the most beautiful scenic roads in the world—Lahaina's famous Front Street, and many more.

"There is already a pleasant, calm, and positive atmosphere in the airport," Melanie said to her husband.

Inspired by this atmosphere, Melanie could have danced for joy. She felt like this was exactly where she belonged. It was early in the evening. The family finally wanted to get out of the airport. But first, they had to pick up their luggage.

The belt began to move. And the passengers gathered around it. Dirk stood there and wished he could do a little magic because their suitcases were rarely the first on the conveyor belt.

Tired, the family waited to get their suitcases. "I hope the suitcases are there," Melanie prayed and looked at the other passengers. She was never at ease on flights with layovers. With her positive mindset, she simply hoped that her suitcases had found their way onto the right plane. Suitcase after suitcase ran along the conveyor belt. Only hers were not yet in sight.

Melanie was already getting restless, but Lanea put Melanie at ease, "I see your suitcase, Mom."

Melanie was visibly relieved. After all, if her suitcase made it, then the rest of the suitcases would follow after a while. Years ago, each of them had picked out extra obvious suitcases that were very different from the others.

Leilani and Lanea's suitcases were white and had a large, colourful butterfly printed on them. Melanie's suitcase was green and had a large pink orchid printed on it. Dirk's suitcase was plain green. At least his suitcase stood out much better against the masses of black suitcases. Once they had collected their suitcases, they made their way to the car rental counter. It was exceptionally quiet at the counter. They had experienced this differently. A young man in his early 20s quickly completed the paperwork and handed Dirk the key.

Wailuku, their new home, was only 5.2 miles away. The girls ran ahead. They simply ran outside. They felt the sudden heat of 27 degrees. The sun was shining; it was summer. It smelled sweetly of plumeria.

"That's the scent of plumeria," said Melanie. "The flowers grow everywhere in Hawaii! Thanks to their sweet scent, the flowers are also used for making the flower leis, i.e., the typical flower wreaths. It symbolises the beauty and aloha of Hawaii."

"Tell me, Mom, how do you know so much about Hawaii?" Lanea teased her mom.

"I have studied the Hawaiian Islands. One day, I will write a book about you and Hawaii."

"You always have ideas," said Lanea.

In Germany, they had started in mediocre temperatures and heavy rain. The first semester had only just begun. Leilani was a gifted student and moved on to year 5 at secondary school. Lanea had completed the 3rd grade of elementary school with confidence.

There were only a few cabs waiting at the side of the road outside the airport. They didn't see any large buses driving packs of tourists to their hotels just as they knew it from Gran Canaria or other vacation destinations.

They heard the blast of a steam whistle. Immediately afterwards, a locomotive whizzed past them at a leisurely pace.

"Kids, look at the Lahaina Kaanapali & Pacific Railroad. It was once built to transport sugar cane," Dirk explained proudly.

"Nowadays, it serves the purpose of showing visitors the beauty and charm of the island," added Melanie.

"Which one of you will find parking lot no. 30 the fastest?" shouted Dirk.

The girls ran off. Melanie had forbidden them to run in parking lots, but there was nothing going on. So she let them go. Dirk's eyes widened as they entered the parking lot.

"A Chevrolet Blazer in black," whispered Dirk. He was beaming all over his face because he really liked American cars.

"So, do you like it?" Melanie wanted to know.

"It's great! That must be expensive—you really didn't have to. How long has it been rented for?" he asked her.

"One week," she answered happily.

Dirk loaded the suitcases into the huge trunk as the rest of the family got into the car.

"Quick, Dad, please turn on the air conditioning," the girls begged him.

He started the engine, turned on the air conditioning and drove off. Excited and amazed, they drove along the Kaahumanu AVE. The AVE had two and sometimes even three lanes. Road signs allowed them to drive at a speed of 45 mph.

Lush green trees and large palm trees lined the roadsides. The girls put their heads out of the window, enjoying the breeze. They enjoyed the view of the Pacific Ocean with its wonderful colours. The closer they got to Wailuku, the more magnificent the view of the West Maui Mountains became. The sky was bright blue, and large white clouds hung over the mountains. The small town of Wailuku had been growing together with Kahului for several years to form a large settlement area and, as a twin town, represented the capital of Maui in the north of the island.

Kahului and Wailuku are the economic centre of Maui and are home to about 60,000 inhabitants. This is where real Hawaiian life takes place. While Kahului, with its large airport and huge malls on the coast, is more of a faceless prefab town that was hastily built around 1950 for the numerous plantation workers, the older Wailuku at the foothills of the West Maui Mountains shines with more charm.

"Why this island? Why not Kauai or Oahu?" the girls asked their parents curiously.

"Maui is the second largest island of Hawaii and is known for its activities and breathtaking landscapes.

This island has become world-famous for its beaches, the holy Iao Valley State Park, the humpback whales, the farm-to-table cuisine (seasonal food), and the beautiful sunrises and sunsets on Haleakala and Road to Hana. Besides, your father and I got married here," Melanie explained to them.

"Stop the car!" Melanie suddenly shouted.

Dirk was startled, looked in the rear-view mirror, and pulled over. The girls had also flinched.

"I didn't mean to scare you," she apologised to her family. They got out and looked at a famous mural of an old Hawaiian woman in a yellow dress with a wreath of flowers on her head, squatting opposite a Hawaiian girl by a river.

"You know, children, this picture has a special sign and tells a story about the town of Wailuku. It tells about the sugar cane plantations of the islands and the importance of water, taro and the Nā Wai 'Ehā (Four Great Waters) in the West Maui Mountains."

When Melanie was done with her history lesson, the family got back in the car. Leilani and Lanea were bursting with curiosity because they would finally see the house they had only seen in pictures so far. They turned right into a driveway that was about 20 metres long. Large palm trees, banana trees, and many colourful flowers protruded from the green areas. They drove slowly towards a two-storey green and white plantation-style cottage. It had a covered porch that ran around it and was furnished with bamboo furniture.

The house was located at the end of Waiehu Beach. Because of this, a piece of private beach belonged to the property. Dirk parked the car in front of the double garage, and the girls quickly got out.

"A paradise," the girls shouted. They ran towards the house and pressed their faces firmly against the sun-warmed window panes from outside so that they could look inside.

"Dad, there's an aquarium in the living room," Leilani called out.

"Our green kitchen is ready, too, Mom," Lanea called out. Dirk looked at Melanie incredulously.

"Surprise! I want you to feel at home, too," she whispered to him.

Melanie and Dirk also pressed their faces to the window as a black Dodge van rolled up the driveway. A blonde, cheerful, middle-aged woman got out and greeted the family with a friendly aloha. It was Nicky, their realtor.

"Welcome to Maui; how was your trip?" she asked. "They are beautiful girls," she marvelled.

"Pleased to meet you, but we're pretty tired," said Melanie.

"The furniture is already placed as you asked. We hope you like it. You'll find fruit and snacks in the fridge. Not all of the electrical appliances are connected, though," Nicky told the tired family.

"That's really very nice," said Dirk and thanked Nicky with a friendly *'Mahalo nui loa.'* Nicky handed the girls the front door keys and sat down in her van. "Settle in first. If you need anything, please get in touch with me. The excavator work for your pool will start tomorrow," she called out of the outside window in a friendly manner and continued slowly.

Melanie and Dirk smiled at each other and walked towards the cottage.

"I'll get the suitcases," said Dirk.

But Melanie hadn't even heard that. She marched straight towards the steps that provided direct access to the beach. She took off her sandals and crossed the soft, warm sand until she was standing with her bare feet in the warm Pacific. She looked out at the open, glistening, rough sea. She lifted her head and spread her arms. "A L O H A A A," she shouted in a loud and powerful voice until she ran out of breath. She felt the positive energy inside her. She had missed this feeling and had never been able to feel it anywhere else in this precious world. Her girls ran knee-deep into the water in their long pants and splashed each other with water. Melanie couldn't resist and joined in.

When they were soaked from top to bottom, they saw Dirk standing on the beach, who also looked happy. The girls dashed past him into the house, dripping wet. Now Melanie wanted to have a look at the house, too, and together with Dirk, she went inside. The view from the large panoramic windows of the house was breathtaking. They examined the top floor first. Leilani and Lanea's rooms were not as big as their old rooms, but they were furnished exactly as they had been in Germany. Melanie had their beds, desks, closets, stuffed animals, blankets, and much more transported overseas to create an emotionally safe environment for the girls. The girls also had a small bathroom with a shower for themselves.

Melanie and Dirk's bedroom was downstairs. It was the same size as their old one and was also furnished with their furniture from Germany. There was also a bathroom on the ground floor with a spacious bathtub, shower, and dressing room. The living room was furnished in a modern vintage style, with a large brown leather couch that invited guests to sit together comfortably. A large, thick Berber carpet was designed to create a cozy atmosphere. The wooden floor was antique and, therefore, delicate.

Dirk's aquarium separated the living room from the medium-sized kitchen. He leaned against his aquarium, which Melanie had brought over from Germany, and watched his fish. Melanie had it transported by air by a specialised animal transport company. His fish had survived the long journey. He had lovingly raised them for years. That was his hobby. Although Melanie loved water, she couldn't share his joy in it. She liked looking at the colourful fish but nothing more.

She had never had to clean one of his aquariums. Everyone had their hobby. She had used Facetime to tell the moving company exactly where the furniture should be placed. That was very exhausting for her because when the men were working, it was already late at night in Germany. But their work and effort had paid off.

The porch was furnished with a huge seating lounge made of wooden pallets, cozy cushions, and blankets. As well as an awning hung with colourful solar lanterns and a high-quality barbecue grill. From there, they had a good view of their green garden lined with palm trees, where their pool would soon invite them to splash around and cool off. Melanie went to find the girls in their rooms as she wanted to put their clothes away. Leilani and Lanea were lying on the bed in Leilani's room, looking out of the big picture window at the open sea.

"And children, what do you think?" Melanie asked them as she snuggled up between her girls.

They both snuggled up to her and were satisfied.

"Get some rest first! I'll put the clothes in the closets and get us something to eat."

"What's the Wi-Fi password?" Lanea asked her, holding her cell phone in her hand.

"There's no Wi-Fi here," she said and grinned at her girls. She grinned so exaggeratedly that the children didn't buy it.

"The password is ALOHA2023," Melanie told them.

She quickly put everything away. She was completely exhausted from lack of sleep.

Dirk came out of the garage. "The dirt bikes, skateboards, bicycles, the power pack, the canoe, and the fridges are flawless at first glance, but your surfboards are—" he pointed out quizzically.

Melanie opened her eyes and dashed past him into the garage. They were lined up nicely against the wall. She shot Dirk a dirty look to let him know that she wasn't joking. Dirk laughed out loud.

"That's not funny," she hissed at him.

Then she left him. "I'm just going shopping in town," Melanie called while closing the door behind her. She enjoyed the drive under the palm trees with a view of the sea and the bright colours of the volcanic forests. She felt at home. Did she already feel a sense of longing for her Hawaiian family, none of whom she knew except her father? She had imagined her grandparents a thousand times. She only knew that their names were Haumea and Ku and that they probably lived on Kauai—*if they were still alive* because she didn't know that either. Dirk took the opportunity to connect all the electrical appliances in the house.

"The most important thing is the TV," he said to the girls as they clattered down the stairs and helped him with his work.

Shortly after they had plugged everything in and settled down in front of the TV, Melanie returned from her shopping trip.

"What's the point? There are no German channels here," he said and switched the TV off again.

Melanie had bought fresh mahi mahi fish for the barbecue, some potatoes, and bread. "The mahi mahi fish is incredibly juicy and full of flavours," Melanie sold it to her girls in a tasty way. She was impressed that the girls definitely wanted to try it. Dirk fired up the barbecue. He was also the best barbecue master in the eyes of the girls. And he always made it his job to serve a delightful meal. Melanie prepared the fish in the spacious, mint-coloured kitchen she had brought with her from Germany. She had even had the granite surfaces transported by sea. The kitchen was too new to be left there. Before falling tiredly into bed, they happily grilled the fish and ate for the first time in their new home on the cosy porch, with a dreamlike view of the sunset and its flaming clouds.

THE SURF SCHOOL

"Aloha. Get up, kids!" they heard their mother shout. Leilani and Lanea woke up together in one bed once again.

"Have you slept together again? I can't imagine you had a decent night's sleep," Melanie grumbled to them up the stairs.

Leilani and Lanea had always slept together, even though they had separate childhood rooms.

"That's how it is between sisters," one of the girls called sleepily to her mother. Lanea grinned gloatingly at Leilani. They both hopped out of bed, put on shorts and shirts, and trampled down the steep stairs. Dirk was already outside, coordinating the pool work.

"You've slept late, it's already 11 a.m. We have to be at the surf school in an hour. We'll get the key and everything explained there," Melanie said.

"Have breakfast, and don't forget to apply sunscreen. The sun here is very strong."

"How boring," said Leilani, looking out into the green garden.

Lanea winked at her sister and whispered, "Let's go surfing then!"

"Are you crazy? Mom wouldn't allow that. We don't know the conditions."

"Why are you always such a scaredy-cat? She's busy; if we argue well, she'll let us. Come on, put on your bathing suit."

Leilani was in a jam, but she also wanted to surf. With a queasy feeling, she put on her blue bikini after all.

"Then let's get our surfboards quickly," Lanea called out as Dirk and Melanie sat on the porch with a cup of coffee and looked out to sea.

"You want to go out on the water today already?" asked Melanie, a little worried.

"Yes," Leilani and Lanea answered at the same time.

"Now that we're here, we can surf every day. That's what you said to us," Lanea affirmed, looking at her father.

"We don't know the conditions at the spot. You're not going out there without me. Have you checked the wave period yet?" replied Melanie.

Leilani and Lanea pulled their sweet faces.

"Mom, you've dragged us to every beach for the last seven years with endless surf lessons. We know what to look out for. Please don't worry. In Zarautz, you told us that you would let us out on our own from now on," Lanea defended herself.

"But not at a new surf spot." Melanie thought about it for a moment and said, "The Atlantic is different from the Pacific! The ocean is much more powerful than you and I, so we have to respect the force it brings with it. The more you know about the ocean, the currents, and the waves, the safer you are out there. So please take some time to study and observe the conditions. Are there any dangers? Are the waves strong? Are there strong currents?" Melanie reminded her girls.

Leilani interrupted her mother and chimed in, "Or we'll just ask the locals."

"If my English is good enough," Lanea exclaimed, a little disappointed and looked down at the ground sadly.

"I'm sure you can communicate that in English. We'll ask the locals straight away. You can often see from other surfers which areas are safe," Dirk cheered his girls up sympathetically.

The girls were delighted, ran into the garage, and stood in front of their surfboards.

"Which one are you taking?" Leilani looked at her sister curiously.

"I'll take the short. And you?"

"I'm going to try the Malibu today."

Melanie stepped behind her. "A good choice. Why not the fish or longboard?"

The girls thought about it and replied: "We can dance up and down on the long; the wave period is too short for that, and the fish picks up an incredible amount of speed. It would be too dangerous as we don't know the spot."

Melanie clapped her hands happily and walked with them towards the beach.

Dirk waited on the beach and enjoyed the view of the boats slowly sailing past on the horizon. Leilani and Lanea put their surfboards under their arms and walked along the beach with their parents towards the surf school.

They were curious about the surf school, which they had only ever seen in pictures. They thought Melanie had bought it for very little money. The surf school was small but right on the beach and only 300 metres from their beach house. The closer they got to the surf school, the more crowded and lively the beach became. As it was Sunday, the beach was also busier than during the week. Melanie loved watching people on the beach. The atmosphere fascinated her again and again. Tourists often gave themselves away by their red sunburnt skin, their exaggerated layers of sunscreen applied to their skin, and their '*I Love Hawaii*' shirts. The locals usually wore head protection and played and splashed around in the water with their children. Surfboards of different colours and varieties lay around in the sand.

Surfers sat on their surfboards and enjoyed the line-up view. The line-up is the entirety of surfers sitting on their boards in the water, waiting for the waves to roll in. It is the point in the surf where the waves form the optimal shape for surfers to stand up and rush down into the wave trough. It was one of those days when the waves had to be taken advantage of. An incredible number of upper bodies flashed out of the water. Graceful and full of elegance, women, men, and children danced the hula with flower-decorated hair, colourful flower leis, and bamboo skirts around their hips, with small steps and hip movements to the music.

The family stopped and watched them with great interest. They expressed their *joie de vivre* through hula dancing. Hula dancing was regarded as an art form that had its roots in traditional ceremonies and had been practised since time immemorial. The accompanying dances and songs were centuries, perhaps millennia old. They were passed down from generation to generation. The chants represented a connection between humans and the goddesses and gods. A connection was also made to the stars and ancestors. Some texts were a kind of prayer or song of gratitude.

"Are your eyes about to fall out?" Melanie asked her husband in a funny but slightly chastising tone.

Melanie hadn't realised that she was already standing in front of the surf school. The hula dancers were certainly not entirely innocent in this happenstance.

"I've never seen such a beautiful surf school," Lanea said wholeheartedly.

"I honestly haven't either," Melanie breathed in amazement.

The surf school was about 100 square metres in size, built on one level from bamboo, and covered with a thatched roof.

"It's like a beach bar," remarked Dirk.

"The beach bar is not far away. Look!" Melanie pointed to a small, blue-painted wooden hut next to the surf school. "Look, there's Kaleo on the beach," Melanie said, spotting Kaleo.

An older man in his mid-60s was instructing four people standing on the shore. Their surfboards were positioned on the sand in front of them, and they were doing the usual dry runs on the surfboards.

Kaleo was stocky and muscular. At 1.75 metres, with his long, curly brown hair and bright brown eyes, he looked a lot like Maui, the demigod. Hawaiian tattoos adorned his body from the neck down. Dirk introduced himself to the owner of the beach bar. They seemed to get on well straight away, Melanie noticed. He was around the same age, of medium height, and had long blond hair. He wore a Western-style straw hat on his head.

Leilani and Lanea sat down on the lounge in front of the surf school and watched their mom's steps. Melanie went to the shore and introduced herself. When the surf instructor recognised her, he also greeted her with an aloha and a firm hug.

"Great, you've made it," he said happily, continuing to hold her by the arms and gazing happily into her face. "How do you like it? I hope I haven't promised too much."

Melanie slowly freed herself from his grip and took a step back.

"We are happy to be here. The spot looks breathtaking. Even better than in the pictures. And the surf school, too."

"As you can see, I still have lessons. I didn't expect you to be here as agreed, and so I accepted the last-minute booking. I hope that's okay with you? Go ahead and have a look around. What about your girls? Do they want to go out, too? At least they brought their surfboards," he said in a benevolent voice.

"I actually told them not to because we don't know the conditions."

"Listen, anyone can surf here today. There's only sand here. A little further ahead," he pointed with his right finger in the direction of her house, "that's where you have to be careful."

Melanie waved to her girls over, and they both came sprinting towards her.

Leilani stepped forward. "I'm Leilani."

Then Lanea stepped forward. "I'm Lanea."

They looked expectantly at Melanie. Melanie nodded and smiled.

"Please get some surf shirts from the clothes rails in front of the school. That way, I can recognise you better out on the water," he told the girls.

They dashed off, pulling on pink Lycra surf shirts with the name '*Kaleo's Surfschool*' written on them.

Kaleo's group consisted of two blonde teenage American girls aged 16 and two teenage Hawaiians aged 13 to 14.

"Aloha," they greeted each other. The girls laughed a little at Leilani and Lanea. They thought they were just too young to surf.

After the typical warm-up, Leilani, Lanea, Kaleo, and the rest of the group went out onto the water.

"Cold," they all remarked.

However, the deeper they went into the ocean and the more waves they broke through, the warmer they became. The 16-year-old girls had the water splashing violently in their faces because they didn't understand that they had to dive under the towering waves. The rest of them were comfortably sitting on their surfboards and waiting in the line-up. Now, the two blondes had also left the oncoming waves behind them and were sitting in the line-up, where the waves rolled in beneath them.

Leilani and Lanea were sitting on their surfboards, dangling their legs in the water and chatting cheerfully with the boys. Kaleo had his hands full with the two blonde girls.

Melanie and Dirk sat on the beach and watched them. Melanie was overcome by an uncanny tiredness; it was the jet lag catching up with her. She actually wanted to go out onto the ocean, but she was just too tired. The man from the beach bar tapped Dirk on the shoulder and offered them a non-alcoholic cocktail. They were both delighted and took the cocktails from the tray. As Melanie sipped her cocktail, she took out her cell phone and checked the wave period on her app. The wave period was 15 seconds. This meant that the waves had plenty of time to organise and build up.

The wave height was around 1.5 metres. Due to the wave period, the waves could get even higher, Melanie explained to her husband. But Dirk just looked at her, disinterested and slurping with a squint. She realised immediately that he wasn't actually listening to her.

He looks kind of tired, too, she thought.

But she kept it to herself. Dirk had tried surfing once before, but it hadn't gotten him like it had her. He was already through with the subject when he had to squeeze into a wetsuit for the first time.

When Melanie taught her girls to surf, she always made sure that the wave periods were very long and the waves were not too high. Otherwise, it would have taken the fun out of it. When she took them out into rougher surf, she always booked a surf instructor to accompany them. It was impossible to look after two water lovers at the same time.

When she took a trip with her girls to the coast of Biscay in Spain last fall, the two of them proved their safety on the surfboard and their understanding of the sea. She was insanely proud of them. Melanie was sure that a quarter of Hawaiian blood bubbling in their veins was the reason for their passion and longing for the sea. They were brave. They always radiated warmth and joy. They reminded Melanie of the Polynesians who crossed the Pacific on self-built rafts. Because they also followed their hearts. Stars eventually led them to the beautiful volcanic islands.

Melanie looked towards the sea and saw her girls riding the wave smoothly almost all the way up to their feet. They jumped off the surfboard and showed the hang loose sign. They always did this when they had completely surfed a wave. The look on Kaleo's face suggested that he was impressed by them. Finally, he also came surfing up with his longboard, on which he danced up and down. He was an absolute pro. He looked like a king whose kingdom was the sea. He jumped off the board and ran towards the family.

"I've rarely seen anything like it. At such a young age, you already have such great posture and tricks on the surfboard. If you keep practising, I'm sure you'll make it to the next competition here on the beach in three weeks' time. Sign up for surfing lessons at school," Kaleo begged a little.

Leilani's and Lanea's eyes widened even more, soon followed by a cheeky grin. They wiggled their eyebrows comically. Their faces were already a little red from the sun.

"Have you got sunstroke, or why are you looking so funny?" Melanie teased her girls.

"We'll think about it. Thanks, Kaleo, for the compliment."

"Would you like to help the two blonde girls? They are complete beginners. You can show them the pop-up and what to look out for while doing it so they don't fall into the water," he pleaded a little.

They grinned at him and threw themselves into the ocean, beaming with joy.

"Don't get cocky now," Melanie called after them.

The students lay on their boards. Lanea and Leilani held onto the back of the surfboard. As the wave rolled in, they gave them a quick push as they didn't manage to paddle out straight away. They lined up and hurtled down the wave. One of them managed to stay on her feet for a moment, but when the wave broke, she lost her balance and crashed into the water. The other girl hadn't managed to get up, but she enjoyed the ride on the wave lying down.

"Another way to do it," the girls thought out loud. They repeated this a few more times.

"Practice makes perfect," Leilani said to them.

Together, the girls had a lot of fun in the water.

In the meantime, Melanie had already gone to the surf school with Kaleo. Kaleo was born in Hawaii and took over his father's surf school. He was, therefore, able to learn to surf as a young child. Kaleo won the title of '*Maui Surf League Champion*' in 1990. With the money he won there, he was able to keep his head above water for years.

"The surf school needs new paint here and there. Then it will look almost like new again," Kaleo remarked. "The saltwater eats away at certain surfaces," he continued.

Kaleo spent hours a day in the water teaching; how could he have had the time and energy to renovate the school? His wife had died of coronavirus two years ago, as she had already been ill for some time. His son lived in New York and rarely came to visit him.

He called the surf school 'Kaleo's Surfschool.' Melanie found the name suitable and kept it. The name had been known for decades anyway. For historical and business reasons, it made no sense for her to change the name. She had long dreamed of opening her own surf school. With the help of her husband, who was a very talented craftsman, they would manage to give the surf school a new shine.

They entered a large lobby with a reception desk, a computer, and a cash register. There, Kaleo offered many accessories for sale. Homemade shell necklaces, bracelets, caps, swimwear, T-shirts, shorts, and towels.

"Where do you get all the wonderful accessories from? How lovingly they've been designed..." Melanie asked him.

"Katy, an old friend from Oahu, makes some of the accessories herself and actually sells them in almost all surf schools on the Hawaiian islands. She comes to visit once a month. If you need them, I'll give you her number."

"Fantastic, I absolutely have to meet her," she told him.

Kaleo's eyes suddenly shone, and she realised that Katy was dear to him. At the back, there was a large changing room with a separate shower room and toilets, as well as a storage area where surfboards in the colours white, pink, Caribbean blue, and yellow were stored. Kaleo had given upmost importance to quality. He offered surfboards made of various materials, such as polyurethane foam with polyester resin and expanded polystyrene foam with epoxy resin. In front of the surf school, there were clothes racks for wetsuits and lycra shirts to dry, a water hose, and three water basins for cleaning the wetsuits and lycra shirts. Surfboards for daily rental were right next to them. Melanie had been in contact with Kaleo for months. She knew how the surf school worked, thanks to her frequent e-mail correspondence with Kaleo. But he had never told her about Katy and the accessories.

"It's a good thing I hired him part-time," she mumbled to herself because she was due to start next week. She had already looked at a few surf schools, but this one was by far the most beautiful. In Melanie's experience, there were hardly any surf schools directly on the beach.

Most owners of beachfront buildings usually only rent out their premises to restaurant, supermarkets, and souvenir operators. The revenue is simply more lucrative than for a surf school. This is also the reason why surf students are often driven from the center to the top spots in minibuses. However, this sometimes meant a lot of lugging around. In this case, Kaleo's father had inherited and run the surf school for generations. However, as his son lived in New York and wanted nothing to do with the surf school, he was forced to sell it.

It's a shame if there's no interest from those who come after us, thought Melanie. But it was to her and her family's advantage.

Here and there, some repainting was needed, or some tiles had to be replaced, but overall, there was nothing her husband couldn't do.

Kaleo handed Melanie a timetable showing the days Monday to Sunday. Classes for elementary and middle school students were scheduled for Monday, Wednesday, and Friday from 11 am to 3 p.m., with Tuesday off. Saturday and Sunday rental and lessons on request from 11 am to 4 p.m.

"Just the way I like it," Melanie grinned.

"I sent you the price list. Would you like to change it?" Kaleo asked Melanie with a serious look.

"I compared them with the European surf schools. You're well below them, to be honest. I've drawn up a new price list. I've already sent it to the schools in the hope that the students will be allowed to continue in surfing lessons."

"Let's see what the locals have to say," Dirk remarked and joined them. "Well, what would they do if they needed surfing equipment or wanted to give tourists lessons on Hawaii's dream beaches? Then they have no choice but to accept the prices."

They stepped out of the surf school and looked for their girls, who were talking in the line-up with two dark- haired girls on their surfboards. Lanea managed to surf all the way down the wave. Leilani lost her balance and fell into the rolling wave. Her surfboard came shooting up vertically out of the wave. Along the leash, her foot flashed briefly out of the water.

She must have swallowed a lot of water while she was being thrown around under the surface.

"Poor thing," Melanie murmured and felt for her. But when she saw that she came up and plunged into the waves again, she was reassured.

In a way, she could rest easy, because the special thing about this stretch of beach was that there were no reefs or rocks in the water. If there had been, she could have injured herself. Leilani came out of the water with a dripping nose. Lanea and the two girls followed her.

Kaleo's group was sitting on the beach and was visibly exhausted from battling the waves. The constant paddling made their arms tired, and the sore muscles were pre-programmed.

Leilani introduced the two girls to her parents.

"This is Kiana and Kalea," Leilani told her parents with a little excitement. She then continued, "They are eleven years old and twin sisters."

They were real Hawaiian girls, with their long, thick, dark brown hair braided into a plait, their big eyes, and their tanned skin. They looked so much alike. The only thing that made them different was the colour of their eyes. Kiana had green eyes, and Kalea had dark brown eyes. They both wore a bright yellow bikini.

Melanie fell in love with them straight away. "They look a lot like our girls," she noticed.

"They go to the elementary school here in Wailuku. They were born in Kauai but moved to Maui because of their parents' work. They live in Lahaina, the famous whaling village," Lanea told them.

"Nice to meet you," Melanie said happily.

Kaleo's group had just showered and had already changed. The blonde Americans thanked Leilani and

Lanea for their support in the water and headed towards the beach bar.

The Hawaiian boys approached the family and introduced themselves.

"We are James and Jones. Our house is in a small village a mile from here. Our parents own a hotel in Oahu. We were born on the Big Island. It's the biggest of the islands. If you ever want to take a trip there, we'd be happy to accompany you."

Melanie and Dirk thought that was very nice and would certainly consider the offer one day because, so far, they had visited all the islands except the Big Island. There was no particular reason for it. They hadn't managed it due to time constraints.

"If you would like to take a trip to Kauai, we would be happy to accompany you there," added the twin sisters.

They all laughed out loud.

Melanie and Dirk were grateful for the friendly welcome they received from the children. They were delighted with the hospitality and open attitude.

Most of all, they were pleased that the girls were already making friends.

Now, the jet lag was also catching up with the girls. They took a long shower. It seemed like half an eternity to Melanie, and she waited in the air-conditioned surf school. But her girls didn't want to go home yet and arranged to meet up with the twin sisters.

"Go on, kids," said Dirk. "You'll be home by 7 p.m., please." The parents said goodbye to Kaleo and the rest and went back to their beach hut together. Melanie told Dirk about her ideas for the surf school. She had planned to set up an online store to sell beautiful surfing articles. She was thrilled with the twin sisters and James and Jones and couldn't believe she was the owner of Kaleo's surf school.

CULTURE HAWAII

There was a cool bag on the porch. Curious, she placed the bag in front of her and opened it. It was poke, a Hawaiian dish. The fish is marinated with soy sauce, sesame seeds, and various spices and then mixed with vegetables. Poi is one of the most important Hawaiian staple foods and is made by pounding the boiled (or baked or steamed) tubers into a chewy mass. Kalua pork is a typical Hawaiian dish. Traditionally, kalua pork in Hawaii is prepared in an imu, an earth oven.

"Who thought of us? So lovingly prepared..." Dirk asked Melanie, looking at her in awe.

"Surely Nicky, the real estate agent. I was a little surprised at how quickly she headed off again. But it was a great gesture!" she said.

Melanie and Dirk took a look at the earthworks. Half of the pool hole had already been dug. Dirk and the girls wanted a pool. They planned a pool that was 1.5 metres deep, 4 metres wide, and 6 metres long.

In the evening, Leilani and Lanea arrived on time for dinner. They really wanted to show their new friends their new beach house.

"Feel free to stay for dinner. Then you can tell us a bit about Hawaiian culture," Melanie asked of them.

The twins seemed excited and sat down. They said that they also lived in a house right on the beach on the famous Front Street. And their parents ran a restaurant in their beach house. They told the family that they were proud of their culture.

"In Hawaii, people always greet each other with 'Aloha,' which should always be returned with a friendly 'Aloha,'" said Kiana cheerfully.

"You should also memorise 'Mahalo,' which means 'thank you,' and 'Kapu,' which means 'forbidden,'" Kalea affirmed.

They said that disrespect and unfriendliness are frowned upon among the people of Hawaii. And that Aloha's cosmopolitan understanding of life demands respect for all people, races, religions, and views of life.

Showing respect and mindfulness towards nature and divine creation at all times was what made Hawaii the most environmentally friendly state in the USA.

Melanie added that the culture of the inhabitants of Hawaii could be summarised as the aloha spirit and that this already shaped the social and societal basis of the native Hawaiians and prevailed to this day despite the multi-ethnic mixture.

"Aloha commands appreciation, kindness, and goodness and is taught and lived in the ohana, the family," Melanie emphasised.

"Our mother is also of Hawaiian descent," the girls called out to the group when they heard a honk. The twin sisters packed their bags and went out the door. The rest followed them. A man with a bald head and a long gray beard got out of his black van and limped towards them. His arms were completely covered in Hawaiian tattoos.

"Grandpa," the twin sisters called out to him.

He greeted the family with an extremely friendly aloha.

"Aloha," Melanie replied and introduced herself and her family.

"I'm Lono Binkom," the grandfather said, introducing himself. Had Melanie understood correctly? Lono Binkom? He had the same birth name as her. She remembered that her mother had once told her the first names of her father's brothers. It had been so long ago that she had only remembered this name. The twin sisters got in. Melanie dove back into her thoughts while Dirk talked to him about the beach house. When Melanie regained consciousness, she spoke to the twin girls through the open window: "You are always welcome."

Lono got into the car and thanked them with a 'Mahalo,' which meant thank you.

"Your granddaughters are sweet as sugar," she said to him through the open car window. They said goodbye with a hearty 'Aloha' and drove off slowly.

The girls had their first day at school tomorrow. Melanie could see the tiredness in their almond-shaped eyes.

They barely managed to stay on their feet, so Melanie quickly put them to bed. On the terrace with a cool drink, Melanie and Dirk talked about the grandfather's name.

"I'm sure many people are called Binkom in Hawaii," they mused to themselves.

"Is it a coincidence, or is it really my father's brother? The age and the name obviously fit. Oh God, he does look like him!" Melanie fiddled, biting her nails slightly.

At least he also had one of the names of the four main gods, like her father. The name Lono reminded her of a Hawaiian myth. He was the god of fertility and agriculture who descended to earth on a rainbow. In agriculture and in the planting tradition, Lono was equated with rain and nourishing plants.

Dirk had already gone to bed while she was still sitting on the lounge on the porch. As she dozed off there, looking at the starry sky, she struggled with the thought of not paying any attention to the matter yet. It was too early. She wanted to take care of her family right now when everything was still new for her girls. She wasn't ready to deal with any unknown relatives just yet and enjoyed the warm evening air.

SCHOOL

Early in the morning, Leilani and Lanea got ready for school. They got dressed up and put on dark blue shorts, white shirts, and sandals.

Melanie had prepared their school bags and lunch boxes. Dirk was sitting at the breakfast table, and the girls joined him, well-rested.

"Dad, where's Mom?" the girls asked him quite quickly.

Dirk rolled his eyes and pointed out of the panorama window to the sea. The girls looked in that direction and searched for her between the rolling, glittering waves until they saw her sitting on her surfboard in the reflection of the sunrise. She was sitting about 100 metres away.

Still in her thoughts, she sat there on her favourite surfboard, which was the most beautiful thing, in her opinion. It was white and printed with lots of colourful hibiscus flowers. It was an original from Hawaii. Nobody was allowed to use it except her. She had bought it once on Oahu.

Her gaze was directed towards the island of the valleys, and she enjoyed the view of the white sandy beach, which contrasted with the blue-green shades of the ocean. Rocks were mixed in with the sand. The lush landscape with green rainforests alternating with desert landscapes in various lava formations could be seen in the background. It also had a view of the Haleakalā and the mountains of West Maui. This is how the name 'Island of the Dead' came about. Erosion was responsible for the land bridge between these mountains. As a result, the island looked like a valley.

Melanie let her legs dangle in the water. She loved watching the islands and beaches from the water. She enjoyed the dance of the waves. She was always fascinated by the way the waves built up and broke again. She let her hands glide over the surface of the water.

"This is what Maui looks like from the sea," she whispered, happy that she had made it. But also that her family was doing well so far in the middle of the Pacific.

At that moment, she made a vow not to pay any attention to what had happened last night and not to follow up. She paddled quickly, jumped onto her surfboard, and let herself drift as far as possible.

The school was only three miles away in the direction of Kīhei. They were already late because school started at 8 a.m., and Dirk had gotten lost once. The school building was medium-sized, painted yellow, and had two floors. It was designed for around 300 children. The school had a huge parking lot, sports fields, and a park. They saw the twin sisters and the brothers, James and Jones, standing in front of the school building. Beaming with joy, the children greeted each other with a loud aloha.

"Can you show us the way to the principal's office?" the girls begged their new friends.

They quickly jumped up to the car window, from which Dirk was already sticking his head out to get a quick kiss from his enchanting girls. The girls trotted after the twin sisters and brothers. It was just as they had imagined. Long corridors accompanied by lockers for each child and children of different nationalities running around. Most of the nationalities were Asian, Japanese,

American, and Hawaiian. Some of the boys wore their rugby outfits, as they were used to from American TV series. Some girls wore their cheerleading outfits, and others carried their golf clubs through the bright corridors. They didn't know that from Germany.

Mr William, the principal, greeted the girls warmly in English with an American accent outside his office and invited them into his office. Leilani and Lanea only understood half of what he said. They understood that the school system in the USA was famous worldwide, especially for its high school spirit. A key feature of the education system was that they were all-day schools—operating on a full-day schedule, so students' lives could largely take place at school. As a result, the students and families identified strongly with their school, the sports had a high priority in lessons, and school teams often took part in competitions with other schools.

A girl with long, curly red hair and squinting green eyes entered the director's office and introduced herself as Marty.

"Mrs Lee, my class teacher, sent me to pick up Leilani," she said, stuttering a little.

Leilani jumped up, winked at her sister, and followed Marty outside. Her class was one corridor away. Leilani was totally excited; her little heart was probably pumping more blood through her vessels than normal.

Mrs Lee and the rest of the class greeted Leilani with a special song. Leilani recognised it because her mother sometimes played it on her ukulele. She was even allowed to sit next to Marty. Leilani liked it. She thought briefly about the fact that with Marty's fair skin and red hair, she didn't even come close to fitting into class or in Hawaii at all. Class began, and Leilani focused on her first English lesson at her new school.

Lanea was picked up in person by her new class teacher, Mr Kona.

"Hello," he greeted her.

Lanea was puzzled. Had he actually said hello to her? "Aloha," she replied, and they both laughed from the bottom of their hearts. The ice was broken.

"I thought I'd greet you the way you used to be," he grinned at her. She followed him to her new class. As they entered, the pupils stood up and sang her a welcome song. Lanea's head turned as red as a tomato.

"Mahalo," she said to the class.

Mr Kona pointed to an empty chair, and she sat down. The girl next to her introduced herself as Luana in a whisper. She wore her hair in a long brown ponytail. Her eyes were almost black. She seemed to be an Indian. During lunch recess, the girls were talking, and they immediately realised that they had a lot in common. They were sitting together in the assembly hall and had chosen something tasty from the huge range of dishes on offer.

They were the newcomers from Germany. And they felt that in the looks on the other children's faces. The girls ate lunch together with Marty and Luana. Marty and Luana were appointed as their godparents and showed the girls everything they needed to know. Leilani gave Lanea a cheeky look when she saw James and Jones in their rugby uniforms.

Lanea had a fit of laughter, but she quickly tried to regain her composure after seeing Leilani's expression. It was very embarrassing for her.

"Come and see," they called after the girls as they walked past them. The two gave them a thumbs up.

Dirk was waiting outside for his girls at 3 p.m. on the dot. On the drive home, they both told him about their first day at elementary high school. They all laughed and were now looking forward to a sunny and warm afternoon.

At home, Melanie waited impatiently for her girls and paced back and forth in the kitchen. When she heard the sound of a car engine, she ran towards them, excited and beaming with joy.

"How was your first day?" she wanted to know.

Lanea and Leilani told her that the school was quite modern. It was very different from their old school in Germany, and the children and teachers were very helpful. They told her about the generous range of meals that were offered, from bagels with cheese to scrambled eggs, fruit, pizza, hot dogs, and chips.

"Did you run into Kiana and Kalea?" she asked with a quizzical undertone and a curious look as they sat on the porch, the sound of the excavator's engine deafening their ears.

"They led us to the principal's office."

"Great," Melanie replied cheerfully.

"But, Mom, I only understand half of what the children or teachers say," Leilani said, a little worried.

"It's all in your hands; you have to practise your vocabulary properly," she comforted her children.

They nodded their heads in agreement.

"Can we take part in the surfing competition?" Lanea suddenly asked.

Melanie was silent for a moment until she started talking. "If you stick to all the rules, then I have nothing against it." She hugged her girls tightly.

Dirk had managed to finish digging the hole in the pool and approached his chilling family. "This morning, when I was sitting on the porch, I was able to see a few humpback whales up close," Dirk told them overjoyed.

They all listened to him intently. "During the mating season, they stay among Molokai, Lanai, Maui, and Kaho'olawe until the end of March. The shallow, warm waters around the Hawaiian Islands are extremely popular with the koholā (humpback whales). Humpback whale calves are born in Hawaiian waters and are considered kamaaina (natives). Whales have great cultural significance for the indigenous people. They have been immortalised in ancient petroglyphs on several islands. The return of the koholā (humpback whales) in Hawaii is more like a homecoming than a visit. As some locals believe that the whales are aumakua (protectors of families), the gentle creatures are treated with great respect," he told them. Dirk had seen all the documentaries about whales, sharks, and marine animals.

"You would be the best marine biologist," Lanea complimented.

Lanea and Leilani had already watched many documentaries with Dirk. They loved watching the world of marine animals with him in front of the TV—to Melanie's displeasure because she was the one who had to encourage the girls when she wanted to paddle far out to sea with them. She then succeeded, with difficulty, in taking away their fear of danger in the water and explained to them that it was a safe part of the beach. But as the two of them simply loved the adventure and the freedom of the sea too much, they quickly trusted their Mom again.

"Come on, kids, let's go surfing!" shouted Melanie.

They grabbed their surfboards and set off. At the surf school, they saw Kaleo teaching middle school students. The students were older and wore Lycra shirts that read 'Middle School.'

They quickly tied the leashes around their ankles and paddled out together. First Leilani, then Lanea, and then Melanie. They greeted the other young people sitting in the line-up. Dirk got himself a cool drink at the beach bar and watched the action. The waves were 1.7 metres high and travelling at a speed of 11 seconds. Fantastic sets rolled beneath them. Melanie, Leilani, and Lanea sat on their boards and let their feet dangle in the water while they waited for the perfect wave. They were intoxicated by the breathtaking view around them. All of a sudden, they heard a singing sound. They fell silent and looked into the distance. They heard the blowing of air.

"Humpback whales," whispered Lanea and started paddling very quietly towards Melanie.

The whales were about 50 metres away from them. It was only now that Melanie realised from the look on Leilani's face that they weren't dolphins *but really whales*, and she motioned to Leilani to swim towards her and Lanea. A fairly young whale approached them up to 20 metres. He kept diving under the water and then surfacing again.

Melanie couldn't believe her eyes and asked her girls to paddle out as soon as he came any closer. Leilani and Lanea only moved slowly. They were afraid of frightening the young whale. They knew that young whales were less afraid of humans as they had never experienced whaling before.

Dirk stood on the beach and observed the situation critically. Kiana and Kalea joined him. He was very worried about his family and hoped they would paddle away, but they did not. His hands were tied, so he asked Kaleo for help. Kaleo paddled slowly towards them. It was dangerous to be close to these majestic giants when they threw their flukes up in the air. The humpback whales opened their mouths while the Hawaiian summer sun made their black leather skin glisten.

When Kaleo reached them, the young whale returned to his family, and they disappeared into the distance. The four of them looked at each other and laughed and cried at the same time.

The girls were still very excited. While the waves rolled underneath them towards the beach, Melanie calmed them down for the time being.

"Let's tell Dad."

They got on the boards, paddled and rushed down the wave to the beach together, where Dirk was already waiting for them anxiously.

"Are you all right? I was worried," Dirk asked them excitedly. "Weren't you scared? I could see and hear the humpback whales from here," he blurted out.

Leilani hugged her worried father. Lanea hugged Leilani, and they whispered to him, "It was the best moment of my life, Dad."

Dirk sighed and hugged them both close to him. "I would have loved to have been with you," he whispered back. "But be careful."

They broke away from each other, and the other students came running towards them.

"It was dangerous; our surf instructor told us not to stay, as we were his responsibility," the students affirmed.

"Please tell us everything you've experienced out there," Kalea seethed.

Leilani and Lanea looked pleadingly at their parents, and Melanie and Dirk agreed.

"We'll give you some money; get something at the beach bar. See you at home in two hours," Dirk said to them.

The four of them ran off happily. The parents said goodbye to Kaleo and made their way home. Melanie excitedly told Dirk how she had felt about the huge humpback whales at sea.

Unlike usual, Dirk listened to her with interest. "And you know what, my darling? You don't even know that yet!"

She chuckled, and her eyes widened, "You took pictures?"

He grinned at her and pulled out his cell phone. She jumped for joy. He was always responsible for taking pictures and videos of them. But the fact that he had thought of it at that moment made her happy again.

They sat down together on the porch with a few snacks and looked at the videos and pictures. Melanie cuddled up to him and said, "Honey, the children aren't homesick yet; they're feeling great."

"There's something new to discover here every day."

She agreed with him. He jumped to his feet. "This needs to be celebrated. I'll get us pizza in Kīhei."

Melanie thought it was a wonderful idea.

Leilani and Lanea strolled down the driveway just as Dirk was getting into the car.

"We want to go," Leilani shouted.

"Come in, we're going to Kīhei. Grabbing a pizza."

The girls were already in the car, and Dirk had not even finished his sentence.

"We'll just write Mom a text so she doesn't worry."

They drove south on the HI-30/S. Then down Kīhei Road past Palalau, Kealia Pond National Park, Maalaea Beach, and Sugar Beach through Kenolio Park, and then followed Mai Poina Beach via Ohukai Rd. They knew from their mother's history lessons that Kīhei meant childless and were surprised by the statement when they had already passed several children. Dirk reminisced about fond memories of when he was there years ago with Melanie. They drove past the hotel where they had stayed. They drove along the road where Melanie did her morning laps, and he watched humpback whales on the beach. He remembered their wedding ceremony a few kilometres away.

"Who wants to order?" He looked at his girls as he stopped in front of the pizza place.

Leilani turned her head to the side, and Lanea jumped up. She grabbed the money that Dirk held out, stormed out of the car, and dashed into the pizza place.

Leilani was waiting in the car with Dirk. The air from the air conditioning felt good. They got out of the car while they were waiting and waited for Lanea on the opposite side of the beach. Lanea proudly came out a long time later with four pizzas.

"Next time, you go. Plus, I get to sit at the front now," she said to her sister, Leilani, a little annoyed.

Dirk didn't know her to be that type but left it at that. She got into the car and slammed the door. Dirk and Leilani followed her.

Leilani looked at him and whispered with a laugh, "Maybe she has sunstroke."

Dirk rolled his eyes.

At home, Melanie had set the table outside on the porch. As they ate, Leilani asked around, "Why does Kīhei translate as childless?"

Melanie was surprised and pleased that her children were able to remember a few things from her stories. And she began her history lesson. "The seaside resort on the southwest coast was originally called Kamaóle. Translated as 'childless' in the sense of barren. Due to the low rainfall, it was unthinkable for a long time to grow pineapple plantations or anything similar. The town only experienced an economic upswing when they were able to pipe water from Central and West Maui to Kīhei in the 1950s," Melanie said.

The children were amazed, got up, and left. Melanie was sure that the history lesson was over. She laughed, tidied up, and looked at the sea. She was magically drawn to it. She decided to go out. She quickly put on her red swimsuit, grabbed her longboard from the garage, and a little later, she was dancing up and down the waves with it.

Before going to bed, she went to find her girls in their rooms. The girls were once again snuggled up together in Lanea's bed. They had sent pictures and videos of the whale encounter to their friends in Germany.

"And what are the twin sisters up to? What else did you do earlier?" Melanie asked them as she tidied the room.

"Why do you always ask us about them?" Leilani asked curiously.

"Well, I think they're nice," she replied quietly.

Leilani straightened up and began to talk, "You know the grandfather; what was his name?" She tried to remember the name.

"Lono," Melanie answered her quickly.

"His brother is quite ill. He's stuck in a wheelchair and can't move. The twins and their parents often have to look after him. They don't have much time for the twins, partly because of the restaurant they run. It's a burger restaurant. Maybe we can eat there one day and visit them."

Melanie's heart sank. She thought about the poor sick man because she knew all about sick people. And then she thought about the fact that it could be her father or another uncle of hers who was ill. She should just leave it alone and not ask any more questions. That was what she had decided for herself at sea.

OCEAN SISTERS

On the way to the elementary school building, they met their classmates who had seen or heard about their encounter with the whales. Today, they had to choose a sports course. They could choose from soccer, basketball, cheerleading, gymnastics, tennis, baseball, golf, and surfing. They both decided which course they wanted to take and signed up for surfing lessons. The teachers were delighted with their decision. The surfing lessons took place three times a week.

The time had come: together with the other pupils, Leilani and Lanea took the yellow school bus to the surf school. Their surf instructor, Mr Reves, was a native Hawaiian. He was 1.85 metres tall, athletically built, in his mid-30s, and wore his long, straight black hair tied back in a bun. He was not only a surf instructor but also taught web design and math.

Melanie was already eagerly awaiting the classes. It was her first day as a surf instructor at her own surf school. She had prepared everything. Mr Reves introduced himself and asked about Kaleo. Melanie greeted him and the pupils and told them about the change. She gave Leilani and Lanea a kiss on the nose, which made them happy. Mr Reves and the other pupils looked puzzled. The children disappeared into the changing rooms. Loud screams echoed through the surf school. Mr Reves took Melanie aside and looked her in the face with his almond-shaped grey eyes.

"Are you a native of Germany?" he asked her.

Should she answer him? She would only reveal more information about herself that might be linked to her family—*if she still had one*. Her girls had so far only told the twin sisters, who wouldn't make any further assumptions in that regard. Suddenly, the pupils came running towards them. Melanie encouraged the children to warm up quickly in order to end the conversation with Mr Reves.

There were a total of ten children born in 2013 and 2014. The swell was perfect, 13 seconds, with a wave height of 1.50 metres. Melanie taught the 2013 group in red Lycra shirts, and Mr Reves taught the 2014 group in green Lycra shirts. This made it easier for them to recognise and distinguish the children in the water. After everyone had done their dry runs, they ran into the ocean with their surfboards, beaming with joy. The sky was bright blue, and there wasn't a cloud in the sky.

Some sat in the line-up and enjoyed the view. Others tried to surf as often as possible. Not everyone succeeded. Melanie watched her students carefully so that she could give them tips later. She quickly noticed that Leilani and Lanea did the best of all of them and was surprised. They lived by the sea and were supposed to be much more experienced than her girls. Lanea caught one wave after another. Her style was breathtaking. She paddled hard, looked for the highest peak of the wave, jumped onto her surfboard in one leap, and rode the tube of the wave like a queen. Melanie could see that Leilani took longer to stand up and was, therefore, able to ride the wave more on her knees or not at all.

A girl from her group was adept at paddling or standing up, but she had difficulty keeping her balance.

Every time she stood firmly on the board, she would flap her arms in the air like a parrot and lose her balance.

In Mr Reve's group, Melanie noticed a boy who had difficulty maintaining his body tension and, therefore, often rolled off the surfboard back into the water, lying down. All of this could be practiced because that's what Melanie was there for—to teach others how to surf. It had taken her years to understand what was important on the surfboard. Because they didn't live by the sea, she was only able to build up her skills slowly.

When the lesson was over, the students lay down on the warm sand with their arms spread out like seals. Mr Reves gave the students tips on what they should work on.

"I have to admit, Leilani and Lanea, I'm a huge fan of yours. It's certainly not your first time on the board," he said and looked at Melanie intently.

The girls were delighted with his compliment and briefly listed all the surf spots where they had spent a lot of time in the water with their mom.

"I am fascinated by your nature and your movements. In my eyes, you are ocean sisters. I've rarely seen the ease you have on a surfboard. As if there is only the sea for you."

Some of the students listening to him started to laugh.

"From now on, I'll call you the *Ocean Sisters*. You've got it in your blood. Every year, we take part in the KWL surfing competition. There, we compete with the other schools. This year, the surfing competition will be held on this beach in three weeks' time. I will register you late."

Lanea and Leilani beamed with their now-tanned faces.

"This calls for a celebration," shouted Dirk as he came out of the surf school with a crate of ice-cold drinks. He had overheard the conversation as he was changing a few floor tiles at the surf school. The students sat down in a circle and enjoyed their cold drinks.

Mr Reves began to tell the students how a surfing competition usually works. "Three surfers from three different schools, but from the same age group, in different shirt colours compete against each other in a heat. All three are in the water at the same time and try to surf as many waves as possible in the allotted time."

"How long do you have?" Lanea asked the group.

Mr Reves continued: "You have ten minutes to convince the jury of your skills. For every wave you surf, the jury will give you a score. This usually consists of five people. Ultimately, the scores (points) of the two best waves are added together. The winner of the heat advances to round 3, while the runner-up must first beat other runners-up from other heats in round 2. The third-placed surfer is then immediately eliminated. If a surfer scores a wave in round 2, the other surfers in the heat are given priority. This means that they now have to go first. Of these two surfers, the surfer who arrives in the 'take-off area' first has priority. If the first person in line surfs a wave, priority is transferred to the next person and so on. In order to avoid incidents, accidents, or even injuries, non-compliance with the rules is penalised with hefty penalties.

"For example, there is an interference penalty for 'dropping in,\ which means that the surfer has little chance of progressing. From the quarter-finals onwards, only two opponents surf against each other in a heat until there is a final and a winner."

Melanie summarised once again: "Each wave surfed after a run is rated with points between 1 and 10. At the end of each heat, the scores of the two best waves are added together so you can achieve a maximum of 20 points. At the end of the heat, the surfer with the highest score wins."

"Commitment, degree of difficulty of the maneuvers, innovation and progression of the maneuvers, combination of maneuvers, variation, speed, power, and flow of the run are judged," emphasised Mr Reves.

The sisters remembered the surfing competition they had watched on the coast of Biscay. The beach was full of spectators.

Mr Reves looked at his watch and jumped up. "I think we need to get changed quickly. The bus is waiting," he called out, a little startled.

Dirk introduced himself to Mr Reves while the children changed. Melanie cleaned the sea salt from the wetsuits and lycra shirts and hung them on the clothes racks to dry.

"Dad will pick you up. I have to stay until 5 p.m. Then I'll come home and cook you something delicious."

The children grimaced. "Mom, we have to train. We'll come straight to you after school."

"You'll probably have lunch there, then we'll get a snack right away. See you later."

Mr Reves and the other students said goodbye to Melanie and Dirk with a friendly aloha.

Dirk smiled brightly at Melanie. "The girls seem to be settling in well."

Melanie jumped so hard into his arms that he lost his balance and fell backwards into the sand with her.

LAHAINA

Dirk wanted to explore the island, but above all, he had to find a new car. They had only rented the car for a week.

"Honey, I'm going to do a bit of sightseeing. I'm meeting Kaleo in Kīhei at the pizza place. See you later. I'll bring pizza, of course," he called after Melanie and disappeared.

Melanie looked puzzled, but she was also glad that he was making an appointment. In the distance, she could already see the next group from the other middle school approaching. Melanie had the feeling that it was hotter than usual. She knew that the Hawaiian Islands were tropical. She wished for a rain shower. But even rain showers usually only lasted a few minutes and were then followed by bright sunshine.

Dirk and Kaleo were chatting in the pizza place while their gaze was fixed on Charley Young Beach.

The beach was sparsely populated. They observed families, avid readers, and several snorkelers.

With a bit of luck, they could see swimming sea turtles all along the coast. They talked about the famous Road to Hana. Dirk told Kaleo, a little amused, that when they were there years ago, the many bends, 600 of them in fact, once made Melanie nauseous, and she had to vomit as a result.

On the adventurous and diverse Road to Hana route, they saw breathtaking sandy beaches, rocky shores, pristine white beaches and lush green landscapes, small and large waterfalls, as well as many colourful and rare plants.

A young man in a typical waiter's outfit served them their food. Kaleo knew him. He was a friend of his son.

Dirk found out that they both liked to go deep-sea fishing. Dirk noticed that Kaleo wasn't so relaxed today but seemed a little worried.

What's on his mind? asked Dirk's inner voice.

After enjoying the pizza, they drove to Lahaina together in Kaleo's van. Kaleo told Dirk that it was unusually dry. That the rainfall was decreasing year after year and they were afraid of forest fires. When they reached Lahaina Harbor 21 miles later, Kaleo told Dirk that fishing on Maui was seasonal and that the best areas for deep-sea fishing were off the west coast of Maui. Anglers could catch good prey from May to June, and the sea would be filled with marlin, mahi mahi, tuna, and jacks. Other fish, such as infopacific blue marlin, wahoo (ono), barracuda, and sharks, were also present.

Fishing had a tradition dating back hundreds of years. The early Hawaiians, the first people in the Pacific region, had developed an advanced aquaculture. In the 18th and 19th centuries, the town of Lahaina itself was characterised by whaling, and due to prostitution and excessive alcohol consumption, Lahaina was almost considered a kind of 'red rag.' Several hundred sailors found a safe haven in the port of Lahaina, which was then gradually taken over by missionaries from New England around 1823. The missionaries not only changed the worldview but also established schools and other institutions. The negative image that Lahaina disappeared when the seafarers moved out of the harbour in the following years, and the whaling industry declined.

Even today, the natural town on Maui strives to commemorate the whaling era and educate tourists and locals about its history. Sights, museums, and a variety of places to go out provide entertainment and activities for people from all over the world. Whale-watching tours show how well the whales, especially the humpback whales, are doing on the coast of Maui.

"Do you know the twin sisters Kiana and Kalea? They spend a lot of time at our surf spot," Dirk asked him to distract him from the topic.

"I've known them since they were little. They come to our beach so I can keep an eye on them and because the surfing conditions are the best there. Their parents, Kehaulani and Koa, work in a restaurant on Front Street and don't have time for them. They make the best burger in Lahaina," Kaleo asserted firmly.

"Let's have a cool drink there, and then we'll go home, as I have to pick up the girls," said Dirk moodily.

Kaleo agreed, and they strolled off. They walked past restaurants and stores for a while until Kaleo stopped in front of a 20-metre-high tree. "This tree was planted in 1873. It's a banyan tree," he said.

Dirk was impressed and took a closer look at the tree. The bark was gray and smooth, the irregularly shaped trunk was short and divided into wide spreading branches. The wood was of no economic use as it was soft. Aerial roots sprouted from the lateral branches, which thickened on contact with the ground and supported the crown like a trunk.

The tree covered an area of several hundred square metres. Its roots ran shallowly beneath the surface. The leaves were heart-shaped and leathery. The town told a story of the time of the whalers, the work of the missionaries, and the life of the immigrants on the plantations.

"There it is," shouted Kaleo, pointing brightly to a two-storey cottage on the beach, painted blue and white with a wrap-around porch, which was named 'BINKOM Burger in Paradise' as it was signposted.

Dirk was impressed, and they sat down on the busy porch.

A dark-haired woman in a denim skirt and turquoise blouse, around her late 30s, greeted the two of them with a friendly "Aloha" and held her notepad in her hand. Kaleo introduced her to Dirk. It was Kehaulani, the twin sisters' mother. She looked very pretty and wore her dark hair in a loose braid.

"This is Dirk, the new owner of my surf school."

She happily held out her hand to Dirk and looked at him with her mysterious green eyes. "Our daughters have already told us a lot about you."

"Why don't you come and visit us," Dirk invited them.

"Definitely, but it's not so good at the moment."

Dirk gave her a sympathetic look. They ordered their cool drink. A man promptly served them their drinks. He introduced himself to Dirk as Koa, the father of the twin sisters. Unlike his father, Lono, he looked frail and exhausted. However, like his father, Lono, his arms were covered in Hawaiian tattoos. He wore a black mop of curly hair.

Dirk recognised Lono at the corner of the house, who was in the process of pushing a man in a wheelchair onto the porch. He looked a little sad and patiently handed the man his food spoon by spoon. Dirk had once seen pictures of Melanie's father and wanted to find out if it was him. The man in the wheelchair was wearing a cowboy hat and had his head down so that Dirk couldn't see his face.

"We have to go if you want to be at the school on time," Kaleo interrupted him as he watched. They quickly paid for their drinks and returned to the parking lot.

Dirk couldn't let it go, with his curiosity clinging to him like a limpet. "Can you tell me who the old man in the wheelchair was?" he asked Kaleo as they walked down the street.

"Do you know the twin sisters' grandfather, Lono?"

Dirk nodded.

"It's his older brother, Kāne."

"Lord in heaven, that can't be true!" The realization hit him.

Kaleo was puzzled by his sudden change of expression and continued talking. "He is very ill and has had multiple sclerosis for a long time. As a US soldier, he was often forced to leave his home country and served on various continents around the world. When he came back, he was no longer his old self. I only knew him briefly from old surfing competitions. You should have seen him; he was pretty good at windsurfing. Lono told me a few years ago that he had lived alone in a high-rise building on Oahu for years and had completely isolated himself.

Dirk and Melanie suspected the same thing years ago. A tour guide had found his address for Melanie and left it with her at the hotel. During a small talk on the transfer to Pearl Harbour, she told him his name. He searched for him without her asking him to do so. She decided to look him up. When she followed the address and suddenly found herself standing in front of his apartment door in a run-down tower block in Pearl City, she turned back and swore never to search for him again because he didn't do it either.

"Dirk," Kaleo snapped him out of his thoughts. "What's the matter? Do you know this man?"

"No," he lied to him appeasingly. He wanted to talk to Melanie first. "Kaleo, I have to pick up the children."

"I'll do my best," laughed Kaleo and stepped on the gas pedal.

The children were already waiting anxiously with their godparents, Marty and Luana, outside the school for their father, as he was never late.

"Aloha, Ocean Sisters, come in," Dirk called out to them a little artificially.

The children hadn't noticed and were delighted as they got in.

"Dad, we're meeting Kiana and Kalea at the surf school in a few minutes. We want to go out to sea together and train. Do you think Mom will lend them the boards for free?"

"Listen up, how are we supposed to earn money like this?" he giddily asked them, laughing in a mocking manner.

The girls looked at each other and were amazed at his exaggeration.

Melanie was so happy to finally be able to call it a day. She sat in the cool anteroom and heard the voices of her family coming closer and closer.

There weren't that many visitors on the beach today. Probably because of the heat, thought Dirk, and he stormed into the surf school with his girls and their friends.

"Where's my pizza?" Melanie looked at him, a little disappointed.

Oh, dear, he had forgotten all about that in his shock. The children went out to sea with their friends. Dirk sat down on the sand and put his head between his knees.

When Melanie saw him sitting so forlornly on the beach, she knelt down next to him. "What's wrong? Is something bugging you?" she asked him, totally worried.

"Honey, sit down. I was in Lahaina with Kaleo. He told me a lot about deep-sea fishing and Lahaina. We wanted to have a cold drink at the twin sisters' restaurant. I got to know their parents." Then he wrinkled his nose and continued quietly, "I saw the old sick man sitting in the wheelchair on the porch."

Melanie jumped to her feet and reared up in front of him in a defensive stance. "Don't tell me!" she shouted right in his face.

"But, darling, I have to tell you this. His name is Kāne Binkom. Just as you suspected. He has MS."

Melanie looked at him, speechless and upset. She never wanted to shed a tear for this man, but her tears just started rolling. She felt a burning sensation in her nose; her breaths became longer, and she had to hold her breath. She felt that hopeless emptiness inside her again. As a daughter, she wanted to be with her father in a purely human way, but she was just too disappointed. She was ashamed of what she had wished for him for years. Because that did not resemble the aloha that she lived by. For the sake of her children, she had to remain consistent. She caught herself relatively quickly.

"You said MS," she looked at him with puffy red eyes and sat down next to him again. "If he's in a wheelchair, then he already has muscle failure. Was he able to move?"

"They were sitting further away. Lono handed him something to eat. His head was lowered, and his arms and legs were immobilised."

"Then he already has muscle failure. It could be that he is paralysed from the cervical vertebra onwards. Because MS damages the respiratory function, the nerve fibers in the brain, the eye nerve, and the nerves in the spinal cord. Does Kaleo know that he is my father?"

"No."

"Honey, promise me we won't tell anyone, not even the girls."

"If you don't want me to, I won't tell anyone. But..."

"No, but." She looked at Dirk so harshly that he shuddered. She remembered how the twin sisters used to say that they were born on Kauai. Their father was, too. Now, it turned out that Kiana and Kalea were her long-lost relatives. "I'm going to go home and cook us something delicious. Keep an eye on the children, please. Throw the bags somewhere and lock up. I'll tidy up tomorrow," she said very calmly. She put her sunglasses over her watery eyes and left.

Dirk watched her compassionately and concentrated on the girls.

Over the 300 metres, she reviewed her memories of him. She strolled slowly along the soft ground between the sand and the water running out towards the sunset. Once again, her suspicions were correct. Out of nowhere, she remembered the meanings of the main gods. Her father also had a Hawaiian name for the four main gods. Kāne was the creator and god of light. According to the myths, Kāne lived in a floating cloud between the earth and the sky, located in the west of the

Hawaiian island off the coast of Kauai. It was believed to contain the sacred water of life, whose magical properties included the resurrection of people. Then, the other brother would be called Kanaloa. *That would complete the four main gods of the Binkom family,* Melanie thought.

The choice of name told Melanie a lot about her Hawaiian grandparents. Her mother never told her about her father's family. She probably just wanted to put the time with him behind her. At home, she prepared kalua pork for her family and went to bed early. She heard her girls and Dirk in the kitchen and fell asleep.

STORM

The next morning, Melanie stood in the kitchen, and beaming with joy, she prepared a real American breakfast for the family with fried bacon, sausages, and pancakes with honey. She didn't know what to do with herself that morning and transferred her emptiness into a wonderful breakfast.

As the girls packed their backpacks, she gave them a kiss and whispered the following words to them, as she did every morning: "Dear God—"

"—protect me!" her girls always replied.

It was a ritual she had introduced when the girls started first grade. It was supposed to protect them as soon as they left the house.

"I'll see you on the beach after school. You should train for the surfing competition. It's going to be a great time for you."

"I'm about to drive to a car dealership with Kaleo. Would you like to come with me?" Dirk asked her encouragingly.

"Gladly," she replied. Dirk was a little taken aback, as she usually sought her sea at times like this.

"I don't have to be at the surf school until 11 a.m."

Dirk drove the girls to school. Meanwhile, Kaleo arrived earlier than agreed. He joined Melanie on the porch.

"And what's new?" he asked her irrelevantly.

"Our girls are allowed to take part in the surfing competition in two weeks, as you had already suggested. Mr Reves, their surf instructor, was also impressed by them. He now calls them the Ocean Sisters."

"Honestly, true," Kaleo emphasised with a laugh. He knew him; he was a big boating fan. He came from the business. "Perhaps he is comparing them to the indestructible, powerful cargo ships of a shipping company. The shipping companies often listed their ships under the same initials and called them sisters."

Melanie hadn't expected that. Did Mr Reves really think of freighters when he looked at her girls?

Dirk drove slowly along the driveway, honking his horn. "Let's go," Dirk called out of the window when he arrived.

Kaleo and Melanie smiled at each other and got into the car with him.

"Where are we going?" Melanie asked them from the back row of seats and leaned curiously between the front seats.

"To Kīhei," said Kaleo.

"Great, then I'll get my pizza today," Melanie emphasised reproachfully.

Kaleo looked at her in confusion. "Didn't you have pizza yesterday?"

She looked at him with a shrug, and Kaleo didn't investigate any further. It looked like it was going to be another hot day. She held her head out the window and enjoyed the breeze.

After 20 minutes, they stopped at B&B Auto Sales and Rentals. It was a small, red-painted car dealership with a large glass canopy. In front of the dealership were a few cars of Dirk's liking.

An elderly woman in her early 60s greeted them. Dirk and Kaleo had a lively chat with her. Melanie sat down on an old wooden bench and disappeared into her thoughts again.

A short time later, Dirk tapped her on the shoulder. "So, darling, we're driving a black Dodge Ram now."

Melanie jumped happily into his arms. She could have said that as soon as they arrived which car her husband would choose, but she let him have his fun. After all, she had known him inside and out for 23 years. In Germany, they had also attached great importance to large cars. It was simply always more comfortable and safer in her eyes.

"Kaleo is driving the rental car back to Kahului."

She also knew this quality from him. In Germany, he had his own people for everything. She laughed to herself. How did he always manage that? It was his inept and clever nature.

"That's very nice of you, Kaleo," Melanie praised him.

"I'm going back by train; I've wanted to do that for a long time."

"We're going for a spin." Dirk smiled at Melanie to cheer her up.

"Yes, to the pizza place. I'm so hungry." She hadn't eaten anything since Dirk's message on the beach yesterday.

At the pizza place, Dirk asked her what to do next.

"You are aware that the twin sisters are related to us. They both have the same eye colour as our girls."

"I noticed that when they were standing in front of us for the first time," Melanie agreed.

"Do you want us to pretend that nothing is wrong?" Dirk asked her anxiously.

"I've thought about it, too." That gave her goosebumps because she wanted to meet her family in Hawaii, just for the sake of the children. Maybe her grandparents were still alive. But they decided not to say anything for the time being and to wait and see.

When they had finished their deliberations, Melanie decided to focus on the surf school—how they were accepted by the locals and that the girls would be well prepared for the surfing competition in a week and a half.

"As you wish, my darling," Dirk said and hugged her tightly.

At home, Dirk checked the pool construction site, while Melanie had all sorts of things to do in the ocean with the pupils. It was good that Kaleo was helping her today.

"So many students in one day, Kaleo. How did you do it?" she asked him, a little exhausted.

"With lots of ALOHA. You know that Aloha has a deeper meaning and is much more than just a simple greeting. *ALO* is life, and *HA* means breath—to have a long breath."

She smiled briefly at him. "You're right." Then she went about her work.

The girls came running up to Melanie and called out to her, "We've eaten; our homework is done," and then they tied their leashes around their ankles and disappeared out to sea with Kiana and Kalea.

Melanie was exhausted from teaching all the students, so she let them surf. She cleaned the changing rooms, swept the sand out of the surf school, and cleaned the wetsuits and lycra shirts. She knew what she was getting into. Running a surf school was no walk in the park, but it allowed them to live on the beach. As she stepped out of the surf school, she saw the four beautiful girls sitting on the beach and joined them. She looked at the twin sisters much more warmly than usual. "Are you competing in the surfing competition, too?" Melanie asked them curiously.

"We barely qualified," said Kiana, looking out to sea a little dejectedly.

"That's wonderful. I'm very happy for you," Melanie said to them.

"You are always welcome to borrow surfboards free of charge. No matter what you need. Wax, wetsuits, or Lycra shirts."

The twin sisters hugged her tightly, and Melanie enjoyed their embrace. Then, the girls left again. She stayed seated for the time being and watched the girls out at sea.

"Have you started preparing for the surfing competition yet?" Kaleo asked and sat down next to her.

Melanie looked up at him, startled. "Not yet." But she knew her way around an event and started babbling, "We need the names of the students who want to take part, snacks, drinks, five competition judges, enough sun protection on the beach, advertising posters for the surf school, flyers, a professional video camera, speakers, a microphone, and much more."

Impressed, Kaleo looked at her and nodded with satisfaction.

"I need your help, please," she told him and looked at him with her big, bright brown eyes.

"I'll choose the five judges; that will be difficult enough. And you'll take care of the rest?" he asked her.

"Yes," she replied gratefully.

They watched the children and talked about what the girls still needed to practice. When they came out of the wonderful ocean, after an hour and a half, they sat down with Melanie and Kaleo. He explained to Leilani that she should jump on the surfboard faster. He lay down on the sand and showed her the right movement to be able to jump onto the board faster. She had gotten into the habit of getting up over her knee, and that would take too much time. He explained to Kiana and Kalea that they had to paddle harder because they often missed the wave as a result. He explained to Lanea that she should make herself smaller when she is standing on the surfboard and rushing through the tube of the wave.

"Do you already know who the judges will be?" Lanea suddenly asked.

"I have an idea, but I still have to ask the people," Kaleo answered her. "In any case, we have a lot to do until then."

"It's going to be great," Leilani called out, and the rest listened to her curiously and attentively. "Mum's events are always a hit; she always goes over the top."

Kaleo and the rest laughed from the bottom of their hearts.

"Go take a shower and get changed," Melanie told them. In the meantime, Melanie had put everything away so that she could call it a day. It was getting windier, and the sky was getting darker. "Are you being picked up, children?" she asked the twin sisters.

"Our grandfather will pick us up later."

Melanie was pleased that they stayed for a while longer. They walked through the sand while the waves grew wilder. A thunderstorm brewed over them and forced the girls to run home. Lightning flashed, and it rained cats and dogs. The strong wind made it difficult for them to move forward. The leaves of the palm trees waved violently back and forth.

When they arrived home, soaked, Dirk was already standing in the doorway, worried.

"Come on, kids, dry off first. On the news, they are showing satellite images of a hurricane over the Central Pacific Basin heading southeast towards the Hawaiian Islands. The US airline has stopped air traffic at Kahului Airport.

"Is it going to be bad?" Lanea asked anxiously.

"We don't know that yet. We have to close all the windows and tie everything down because wind speeds of over 200 mph are expected. On the Saffir-Simpson Hurricane Wind Scale, this would correspond to a category 4 hurricane wind speed. They're talking about flooding." Outside, there was heavy lightning, the wind was picking up, and it was pouring rain. All six of them had gathered in the living room on the leather couch.

"Tell your grandfather that you're staying with us overnight. Don't put him in any danger," Melanie ordered the twin sisters.

"Alright," the twin sisters replied. The gusts of wind grew stronger, and the house creaked from all corners. The hailstones crashed so loudly against the windows that they could barely hear each other. Then the light switched off. The girls quickly switched on the flashlight function on their cell phones.

"Honey, look for snacks. Kids, you pack drinks and blankets. We should get in the car. I don't trust this category 4 storm," Dirk said out loud.

The family ran off eagerly, packed everything up, and immediately afterwards, they were sitting huddled together in the car in the double garage. It was pretty cramped, as the car only had room for five people.

"The car is so robustly built that it will protect us from a roof collapse," said Dirk encouragingly. The children snuggled up together in the back seat. Dirk switched on the radio and searched for a station without noise. They listened to the radio. They warned the people in the low-lying areas, including the mega-resorts on the beaches, of severe thunderstorms, destructive gusts of wind, and heavy rainfall that could lead to flooding.

Increasing southern winds would move in from the tropics and cause widespread rainfall with short periods of heavy rainfall over the smaller islands. The heaviest rain would fall just over Oahu and Maui. But this axis of moisture was expected to shift to the east. Dirk and Melanie were relieved at this news.

"*Ohhhh, ohhh, ohhhh,*" rang out from the radio. The song '*Somewhere over the...*' played, and everyone listened to the song and hoped for a rainbow, too. Leilani and Lanea told the twin girls about their lives in Germany. Leilani and Lanea couldn't understand why the twin sisters wanted to visit Germany one day. They had everything here. When the storm subsided, Dirk gave them the all-clear. The girls and Melanie anxiously went to bed. Dirk checked that everything was in order. The light still wouldn't turn on.

Surely the power lines are faulty, he thought and connected his generator from Germany.

The next morning, they looked at the devastation caused by the storm. The waves had come as close as 20 metres to their house. They could tell by the wet sand.

"The waves seem to have been huge," said Melanie.

Fallen palm leaves, coconuts, and objects were lying around in the garden. The driveway also looked desolate, with hardly any plants still in bloom. There were even banana trees in the driveway. They heard on the news that roads were blocked by landslides caused by the heavy rain. No one had yet been killed in the storm. The storm had covered roofs, torn away entire roof ridges, and overturned vehicles. Individual gas, Water, and power lines had been damaged by fallen trees. Emergency services prepared emergency shelters.

The children came down the stairs and had already got ready for school. But Dirk and Melanie told them that the school was not open due to the extent of the damage and that the power had been cut in some parts of Maui and on the other islands. The children only now saw the extent of the storm. They tried in vain to reach the parents of the twins, but no telephone connection could be established. The line was simply dead. The internet connection wasn't working either.

"They warned that the pipes could be damaged by the storm," said Dirk.

As they were cleaning up their driveway, they saw a woman and a man walking down the driveway. It was Kehaulani and Koa. The twin sisters ran into their parents' arms. Kehaulani stroked her girls' heads with relief.

"Are you all right?" the parents asked their twins.

"We are unharmed."

They gathered in the living room and got to know each other better. "We've already heard a lot about you!" the twin sisters' parents told Melanie and Dirk.

Melanie became unsure because she hadn't seen that much of them yet.

"You have Hawaiian roots, the girls told us. Do you also have family here?" asked the mother.

She hadn't expected that now. "I'm afraid I can't say. I've never met my father," Melanie lied to the lady.

In truth, Koa was her cousin. Shouldn't she be overjoyed right now? She wasn't, and she thought of her vow out there on the sea.

"The roof of our restaurant is completely uncovered. The upper floor is destroyed and wet. All the beach houses in a direct beach location have been hit."

Kiana and Kalea started to cry loudly. So loud that Melanie's heart began to bleed.

"The US Army is setting up emergency shelters. We have no electricity, it's really hard at the moment. The restaurant is intact, but our sick uncle is also living there with us. Together with the children, it would be too cramped," Kehaulani said sadly.

"The roads are blocked, so our car is parked two miles away."

"We heard about it on the news," said Dirk.

They were sitting on the big couch in the living room when Melanie had an idea. "Your daughters are welcome to stay with us until everything is repaired."

Koa and Kehaulani looked very grateful and nodded.

"The rest of our family lives on Kauai. It's no problem to accommodate them there, but they would miss too much at school," Koa said.

Melanie insisted; she was determined to offer the twin sisters accommodation because, after all, they were family.

"That's very generous," Kehaulani thanked the family. "Can we help you with anything else?" asked Dirk.

"I can help you with the roof, for example," Dirk offered.

Koa gratefully accepted the offer. "Together with my father, you, and other helpers, we should be able to do this quickly."

"How is Grandpa's brother?" the twin sisters asked their parents anxiously.

They took their daughters on their laps. "He is unharmed and hasn't noticed anything. As you know, his illness has progressed so far that he can neither hear nor see well. He has lost a lot of weight in the last few weeks and is on stronger medication as a result."

"Where is Grandpa?" asked Kiana.

"Your grandfather flew to Kauai earlier. Don't worry, he's fine. His brother needs help on the pineapple plantation."

Melanie listened intently but silently. After a short time, Kehaulani and Koa said goodbye to their girls and the family. Dirk offered them a ride to their car and went with them.

Now, Melanie wanted to see the extent of the damage to the surf school. She set off with the girls.

HAWAII LEI WEDDING

There wasn't a soul on the beach. They found lots of garbage lying on the sandy beach that had been washed up by the sea.

After just a few metres, Melanie could see that the thatched roof of the surf school had held. Melanie and the children were relieved when they arrived at the scene. However, the swell had been so high overnight that the seawater had sloshed into the surf school. The ground was full of clay and sand. There was no point in opening the surf school today or for the next few days, and she set to work with her daughters. Dirk arrived a short time later to help his family. When the surf school was back to normal in the afternoon, Melanie laid four surfboards on the sand. The girls were beaming and quickly changed their clothes.

Meanwhile, Kaleo ran towards Melanie. "Oh, thank God. You are unharmed."

"And you?" Dirk asked him.

"Everything is fine with me. But some people have been hit hard. The parents of the twin sisters were hit. The restaurant is completely covered. The twin sisters are staying with us for the time being."

"That's very kind of you," Kaleo remarked.

The girls came out and got on their surfboards. They warmed up together.

"I'm training you today," Melanie said and approached them. "I'll just get changed, and then I'll join you on the water."

The girls were delighted. They sat in the lineup and were deep in their thoughts when Melanie swam out.

"Without a surfboard, Mom?" Leilani wondered.

"I can train you better without."

Melanie looked out to sea, watched the waves, and called out to them, "Look, there's a set of fantastic waves coming. Come on, lie down, and start paddling."

They lay on their surfboards like cute little sea otters and started paddling slowly. They paddled faster as the waves approached them to get a quicker boost.

"Body tension, chest," she called out to them.

Lanea stood at the highest peak of the wave and roared through her tunnel. Leilani had once again stood up over her knee, losing time and surfing the foaming part of the wave.

The twin sisters were still lying on their surfboards while the waves simply rolled along beneath them. They looked Melanie straight in the face, a little sadly. Now, she wanted to concentrate on the twin sisters. Melanie explained to them that a set usually starts with a small wave, followed by a larger one. At that moment, several helicopters flew over their heads.

The girls held on to their surfboards and watched them. They circled like vultures in the air and filmed the extent of the storm. The girls waved at them. After the twin sisters had also caught some good waves, Melanie ended the lesson for the day.

Dirk had left a message for Melanie and the children, telling them that he had gone to Lahaina with Kaleo to help. Melanie spent the day at the beach with the girls and enjoyed the time with them. The owner of the beach bar gave them snacks and cool drinks.

Although the sun had been shining brightly in the sky for a long time, there were only a handful of tourists on the beach.

They walked home at dusk, happy and carefree.

"Go shower and get dressed. I'll cook us something tasty."

The girls disappeared upstairs.

Melanie prepared a vegetable lasagna, put it in the oven, and then sat down on the lounge on the porch, watched the sun go down, and reflected on the morning. *I wonder who the rest of the family is,* she thought. Now, she missed her mother and siblings very much. Had she left them behind? Suddenly, she received a message on her cell phone.

It was her mother who was asking about them, as she had heard about the storm on the news.

She quickly replied to her.

Melanie: '*Aloha, Mom, we're fine! Our house and school are intact. So far, there are no casualties here in Maui. We have offered friends of the girls a place to stay for the time being, as the roof of their house is completely uncovered. And I have found Kāne!*'

She didn't hear back from her for a while and kept looking at her cell phone. She was too anxious to see what she would say. Just as she was about to go inside, the message tone on her cell phone went off. She leaned back and read the message:

Mom: *'And how are you doing with that?'*

What kind of question was that!? She felt as if a ten-metre-high wave was crashing down on her, pushing her underwater for minutes and spinning her a hundred times like a washing machine. She couldn't describe how she felt. She was on the verge of a nervous breakdown. She was normally never not calm. But the last few days were too much in her bones. She felt like the Hawaiian goddess Pelé—the goddess of fire and volcanoes. In myths, Pelé often appears in the form of a beautiful woman. It was believed that her strong emotions caused volcanoes to erupt. Pelé enjoyed great respect for the Hawaiian Islands. Eruptions were seen as a sign of Pelé's displeasure, which could only be calmed by offerings.

Melanie calmed down without offerings like that and answered her.

Melanie: *'I don't know, Mom. I'll wait and see. He's very ill. He has MS, and his disease has progressed so far that he can hardly hear, see, or move. The storm has taken its toll on us. Talk to you soon.'*

Mom: *'If you need me, I'll come,'* appeared on the display as she placed her cell phone on the table.

Lanea stepped onto the porch and approached Melanie. "Mom, about the storm, is it coming again?"

Melanie hugged her tightly. "Hurricanes get their energy from evaporating water." She looked out to sea. "They form over the ocean, more precisely over the Atlantic or the northern Pacific Ocean. When they go over land, they basically run out of supply and lose strength. However, they are strong enough to cause flooding and strong winds on the coasts. We are well protected here. For people in poorer countries, this poses an enormous risk. They often lack the means to protect themselves adequately from the forces of nature." She paused for a moment. "Dad and I would never let anything happen to you."

Lanea swallowed and looked deep into her mom's eyes. She pressed her cute snub nose to her nose and paused for a few seconds.

"Come on, I think the lasagna is ready."

The rest of the girls came clattering down the stairs, giggling loudly, and sat down at the table. As they all sat at the table with their buns tied up and their faces really came into their own, Melanie noticed the resemblance again.

During the meal, Kiana and Kalea just chattered away. "Our great-grandparents live on Kauai. Together with our uncle Kanaloa."

Melanie's jaw dropped. They had actually named their sons after the main Hawaiian gods.

They went on, "Ku, our great-grandfather, is 91 years old and no longer as fit as he used to be." *That couldn't be true!* "Our great-grandmother's name is Haumea, and at 82, she is still fit and very warm. She helps the poor on the island. They own a papaya farm on Maui, a pineapple farm on Kauai and a particularly large one on the Big Island. Kanaloa looks after a few plantations and several houses on Maui, Kauai, and the Big Island."

"Would you like to hear some old Hawaiian mythology?" Kiana suddenly asked excitedly.

"We often have to listen to this story from them when we visit our great-grandparents," said Kalea, the older one of the two.

The family pricked up their ears eagerly.

"Our great-grandfather was named after the Hawaiian god of war, Ku. Ku was the rising sun and the god of war, on whose favor the outcome of the battle depended. Most sacrifices were made to him. Our grandmother was named after the fertility goddess Haumea. Haumea is the goddess of fertility and birth in Hawaiian mythology. She is the mother of many important deities, including Pelé and Kāne. Haumea is one of the most important Hawaiian gods, and her worship is one of the oldest traditions on the Hawaiian islands. Haumea is said to have given people the ability to give birth naturally. In one story, she visited Muleiula, the daughter of a chieftain, who was experiencing painful labour. Haumea discovered then that humans only give birth by cutting open the mother. When she saw this, she made a potion from the Kanikawi tree, which enabled the mother to deliver the baby naturally."

Melanie, Leilani, and Lanea were speechless for a while.

Melanie had never told them anything about Hawaiian mythology before. She had studied it herself once because she wanted to know whether Tiki figures had a special meaning.

"Mom, your middle name is Muleiula!"

Kiana and Kalea suddenly looked at her in shock and held their breath.

Melanie had only ever dealt with male Hawaiian gods. She remembered her mother telling her that Kāne, her father, really wanted her first name to be Muleiula.

Her mother boycotted him until he agreed to the second name.

The door opened, and it was Dirk. *My husband is reliable*—it flashed through her mind.

He had a knack for popping in at the right moment. But he looked tired and needed to change. His blue shirt, short denim shorts, and white sneakers were completely stained with mud and dust. He walked slowly towards the family and sat down at the table with them.

"Was it very bad?" the girls asked him.

"It's not nice to see this paradise lose its colour overnight. Nature will restore it. But the US Army is doing a pretty good job," he said quietly to them.

"I'll cook you something delicious to eat." Melanie jumped up and whipped up something for him.

The girls went to their rooms and went to sleep.

Dirk and Melanie had snuggled up together on the seating lounge on their porch.

"Tell me, what did you see?" Melanie asked him.

"Roads are filthy from mudslides. Many houses, hotels, stores, and even our pizza spot have been affected. Collapsed walls, uprooted trees, uncovered roofs. I've only ever seen anything like this in movies. I'm not sure if this should be our dream."

Melanie's heart began to race. She suddenly realised how dangerous her dream was for her family. She paused and said nothing at first.

Then Dirk released her with the words, "We'll wait and see."

Relieved at his decision, they went to sleep.

In the days that followed, the children practised their manoeuvres for the surfing competition. Melanie spent a lot of time with the girls and the surf school while Dirk helped set up the roof in Lahaina. The weather was sunny as usual, and the sky was bright blue. Maui was almost as fixed up as they knew it from the catalogues. The US Army withdrew, the power lines were working again, and the surf school was back up and running. The locals and vacationers had recovered. The Binkom family's roof was quickly as good as new, and the twin sisters were able to return to their old home. It was as if nothing had happened. Although Dirk had spent a lot of time with the Binkom family in Lahaina, Melanie didn't ask him about her father. And Dirk didn't say anything to her either.

"The competition will take place in two days," Leilani remarked as she entered the surf school.

Melanie sat in her anteroom and looked at her with a confident expression. "The preparations are underway, my darling," she replied. Melanie had decided to put all her energy into preparing for the competition. She was literally looking for a distraction from her father.

Kaleo had sent her the five names of the competition judges by e-mail. She studied the names and Kanaloa Binkom was also listed—her other uncle from Kauai.

"Well, this is going to be fun," she said to herself. *And why not?* She hadn't met her father's family all her life, and now she was getting to know them all in a short space of time. How long should she carry her secret with her? Would she receive negative protests as a result? From the Hawaiian family or from her girls? She kept her vow.

She sat at her table in the surf school and looked at the lists of participants. Three schools took part. Five grades with three surfers each. She calculated 45 surfers. She reckoned there would be around 800 to 1000 spectators throughout the day. She included parents, siblings, grandparents, tourists, schoolmates, and locals in her calculation. This meant that the beach bar had to provide more than 1000 litres of chilled drinks. And more than 1000 hot dogs and hot dog buns. They needed lots of ketchup and pineapple because many Hawaiians ate their hot dogs with pineapple and curry powder. The hot dog was simply put through three pineapple rings.

As she was about to leave and give her list to the beach bar owner, a Hawaiian woman with a white knee-length dress and short, curly black hair walked through the door.

"How can I help you?" Melanie asked her, puzzled.

The woman held her hand out to her, smiled and replied:

"I'm Katy. A friend of Kaleo's."

That's when Melanie remembered the woman from Oahu. "You sell the beautiful surfing items, right?"

"Yes, that's right," she answered her in the sweetest voice Melanie had ever heard.

"I wanted to ask if you still needed anything?"

Melanie had hardly sold anything in the first few weeks. A few shirts and caps. The stock was still well stocked up.

She shook her head and explained that fewer tourists had come due to the extent of the storm.

And that she wanted to soon implement her idea of setting up an online store selling original surfing products from Hawaii. Katy liked the idea, and they decided that Katy would be their No. 1 supplier.

"But what I absolutely need is a flag that bears the name *'Kaleos Surfschool.'* And that by the day after tomorrow."

Katy looked at her in disbelief. She had to work hard because Melanie wanted to work with her on a different basis soon.

"No problem." Katy smiled at her. "I'll bring it on Sunday."

"Great. Are you a native of Oahu?" Melanie asked Katy curiously.

"I was born in Maui and moved to Honolulu for work. Most customers live in the big city on Oahu," she said a little regretfully.

Melanie had planned to show her girls the island of Oahu after the surfing competition. She wanted to walk with them across the world-famous Waikiki Beach and take them to see Pearl Harbor. The attack on Pearl Harbor, also known as the Raid on Pearl Harbor or Operation AI, was a surprise attack by the Imperial Japanese Naval Air Forces in peacetime on the US Pacific Fleet anchored in Pearl Harbor in the Hawaiian Territory on December 7, 1941. The following day, the USA declared war on the Empire of Japan.

Katy said goodbye to Melanie. She knew that she was in the middle of preparing for the competition. Melanie gave the beach bar owner her list of drinks and food and a price list. She wanted to make sure that the sale was worthwhile. Melanie saw Kaleo jogging towards her.

"Do we have a band? We should have an after-party after the competition," Melanie said to him.

"I used to have an old band. My friend also has the equipment for it. I'll give him a call right away."

"What is your character in this band?"

"Singer."

She didn't think he was capable of that. She would have put him more in the category of fire artist. She imagined him breathing fire with his tattoos on an evening stage.

"What else do we need?" he tore her from her thoughts.

"We need a high seat so that the competition judges can judge undisturbed and have a good view."

"Our competition judges sit under a sun sail at a table on the beach with binoculars."

Melanie was satisfied with that.

"I'll get the table, chairs, and the sun sail."

"Your friend from Oahu was just here; you just missed her."

His bright brown eyes shone again.

"I ordered a flag from her," she said and tapped his shoulder. "You have a flagpole but no flag."

He bowed his head and told Melanie that his wife had raised the flag every morning. He had put it in the coffin to burn as a reminder.

Melanie was now totally embarrassed. "Is it okay for you, Kaleo?"

He nodded to her in understanding.

"She's coming?"

"Yes, she's coming."

"Your competition judges. Where do they all come from?"

"Three are from Maui, one from Kauai, and one from the Big Island."

"Such a long journey for the two of them."

"Kanaloa Binkom has already been world champion on Kauai. He knows the rules of the competition and is keen to cheer on his nieces, the twin sisters. David Kua from the Big Island was also runner-up once and is an old friend of mine who still owes me a favour. The other three from Maui are surf instructors from other parts of Maui. They won't miss a competition." He winked at her and quickly said goodbye.

Melanie sat down on the sand and thought of her uncle Kanaloa, the surfing world champion. She had a lot of respect. Her grandparents had named him after the Hawaiian god of the ocean and the winds. However, his authority and role varied from island group to island group. For the Hawaiians, he was the god of squid, sometimes an octopus, who lived in the depths of the ocean. He was Kāne's younger brother.

"I wonder if he's bringing his family?" she asked herself, tucking her head between her legs and closing her eyes. She enjoyed the sun and the sound of the sea. She heard her girls calling and looked towards them as she lifted her head.

"So, Mom, today is the last training session before our surfing competition. Tomorrow, we'll rest so that we're fit for Sunday. That's what our teacher, Mr Reves, recommended."

"That sounds professional," she said to them and pounced on her girls, cuddling and tickling them both to the ground.

Dirk stood by and smiled happily. "Why so joyful?"

As the children practised in the water, they sat down at the beach bar.

"Do you know who is also acting as a competition judge?"

"No, who?"

"Kanaloa, my father's other brother, who lives on Kauai."

He raised an eyebrow. "I'm sure he wants to watch the twin sisters, or has word gotten around that a half-Hawaiian from Germany is up to mischief on Maui?"

Melanie rolled her eyes.

"I found out that my father's brothers all have the names of the main gods."

"What main gods, are you really crazy now?" he looked at her, frightened.

"Just listen to me," she huffed back a little. "The twin sisters confirmed to us the night you came back from Lahaina that their great-grandmother's name, my grandmother, is Haumea."

"You didn't tell me all that," he said, a little offended.

"Listen. She was the goddess of fertility and helped the Hawaiian chief's daughter, Muleiula, to give birth properly."

Now Dirk's light went on.

"Now, we finally know where the name comes from." *Because the name Muleiula was not on any Hawaiian name lists.*

"When Leilani and Lanea heard the story from the twin sisters, they promptly said that my middle name was the same. They were both startled and held their breath for a moment. Do you think they know who I am? Perhaps their great-grandmother had told them about a granddaughter with that name."

"You should consider just telling them. Tell them you're a relative. Especially for the sake of the children."

Melanie hadn't expected that. He normally stayed out of everything.

"I'm waiting." She kissed him gently on the cheek and mumbled in his ear, "When the surfing competition is over, we'll show our girls Oahu."

Dirk had no objections.

"Honey, I could use some help." She remembered that the surfboards still needed waxing so that the surfers didn't slip off the board. "Make sure the leashes are tied on and clean all the lycra shirts. We need 45 shirts in three different colours."

"That many?"

"We have to expect 1,000 spectators. Could you please help your friend at the beach bar with the drinks and hot dogs on the day of the competition?"

Dirk smiled mischievously at Melanie as he rubbed the wax onto the middle of the surfboards. Of course, there was also a 'cool blonde.'

The girls came out of the sea, relaxed on the sand, and enjoyed the evening sun.

"Are you excited?" Melanie asked them.

"I haven't been able to think about anything else for days. What if I miss the wave and the others are faster?"

said Leilani, a little unsettled, while her sister dreamily tapped the sand with her index finger.

"You'll manage," Lanea reassured her.

"That's easy for you to say. You always make it look so easy. You take every wave. No matter how difficult." Lanea lifted her head and looked her straight in the eye.

"When the wave comes, take your time."

"What do you mean by that?" Leilani asked her in a relaxed tone.

"Well, when you see her roll up and feel her push you forward and roll straight under you, you'll know when it's the right time to get up. At least that's how I do it, and it always works," she encouraged her older sister.

Lanea had developed a great instinct. Melanie was pleased with her instructive insight.

"I'll try again." Leilani stood up and disappeared into the sea.

Dirk had finished his tasks, and Melanie had done everything for the day. They watched Leilani.

"That looks much better," thought the rest of the family.

At home, they freshened up and sat comfortably on the porch. The doorbell rang. It was the twin sisters, their Grandfather Lono, Koa, and Kehaulani. They wanted to thank them for repairing the roof and gave the family a voucher for the restaurant they ran.

"Come in," Melanie asked them. But they had to keep going; the guests and their sick uncle were waiting.

"Are you closing the restaurant on Sunday?"

"We don't open until the evening, so we can watch the surfing competition. Lono's brother, Kanaloa, is coming with his wife and grandchildren. He might even bring his mother," Kehaulani chatted.

"His mother?" Melanie's head throbbed. After 39 years, would she get to meet her grandmother, who she had only recently learned was even still alive and that she had been named after the goddess of fertility?

"Why don't you come to our restaurant afterwards?" Koa invited the family.

"That's very nice, but I think we'll have a lot to do with the dismantling."

"Think about it, we'd be delighted," Lono remarked.

"See you on Sunday," Melanie bid them farewell.

The next day, Melanie decided to keep the surf school closed. She had borrowed a board from her girls and noted on it that the surf school would remain closed due to the competition preparations.

Dirk stood in the living room and gyrated his hips. He always did that when he had a surprise for his girls.

"We've planned a little excursion with you. Please pack your swimming gear, put on sturdy shoes and then get in the car."

His girls looked at him in surprise. "The surfboards too?" they asked him curiously.

"Today is a rest day, no surfboards. Remember your snorkeling gear."

Unlike usual, the girls looked sympathetic and disappeared into their rooms.

Melanie had prepared a cooler bag with snacks and drinks. She could dress up a little today. There was no point in making a great hairstyle out of her hair for surf school. She put on her red swimsuit and her short white summer dress made of light cotton fabric.

A short time later, the family found themselves back in the car. Dirk was amazed at Melanie's choice of clothes, as he had only seen her in wetsuits or lycra shirts.

In the car, the girls were already asking them questions impatiently.

"Where are we going?" Lanea wanted to hear from her father and tapped him on the shoulder from behind.

"We're going to the beach where we got married."

"Paipu Beach!" the girls shouted at the same time.

Paipu Beach was about seven miles from Kīhei. Relaxed, they drove through the interior of the island to the other side and were looking forward to spending time together.

Half an hour later, they arrived at a small parking lot with no view of the beach.

"Where's the beach?" the children started nagging.

"This sandy beach can only be reached via a narrow path through the rainforest. Only the locals and very few others know the way there," Melanie told them.

Adventurously, they marched into the colourful nature of the rainforest and followed a narrow path.

Once they had left the rainforest behind them, all they had to do was climb carefully down a steep slope lined with large and small palm trees. It was one of the most remote beaches in Maui. They had a view of the house of a famous actor, whom they had envied in the past. So they stepped onto the soft, golden sand with lava rock formations at either end of this crescent-shaped beach.

Paipu Beach Park has an excellent reputation for its calm waters and family-friendly atmosphere. The water there offered an incredible marine ecosystem with tropical fish and other marine life that could be observed while snorkelling or diving around the barrier reef. Because of the barrier reef, it was a prime spot for swimming.

In winter, large waves broke against the reef, which protected the swimmers from dangerous currents and high surf. They made themselves comfortable on a picnic blanket that Melanie had spread out. No one else was there but them. Melanie took out the snacks and told her girls exactly how their wedding had gone. Suddenly, they saw a priest in a black robe embroidered with Hawaiian patterns, a blonde woman in a white sequined dress with her fiancé in a blue suit, and a red-haired photographer with her camera strapped to her chest, carefully climbing down the slope. The woman glistened in the sun like a princess with her tiara on her pinned-up wedding hairstyle. The girls jumped overjoyed and sat down on the lava rocks. Melanie joined them on the rocks. They had a better view from there, and the couple were not disturbed. Like Dirk and Melanie, they had decided on a wedding without family and friends.

The priest gracefully held a large conch shell high in the air and blew into it. The white, right-handed conch shell, which is very rare in nature, is particularly valuable. It symbolises the right path and is an object of worship in many cultures. According to their beliefs, the sound of a conch shell drives away evil spirits.

The priest announced the start of the ceremony. The red-haired woman photographed them from all angles.

The priest talked for a long time and spoke to the prospective married couple. They laughed constantly and seemed excited. Then, the wife placed a beautiful flower lei consisting of pink and white orchids around her husband's neck as a sign of love. The husband also placed a flower lei of the same colour around his wife's neck, and they kissed tenderly.

In the past, the couple only exchanged these leis as a sign of love. Wedding rings were first introduced to Hawaii by missionaries at the beginning of the 19th century. Therefore, in today's ceremony, the couple exchanges the flower leis first and the wedding rings at the end.

"How romantic." The family was very touched. It reminded Melanie and Dirk of their own wedding. The newlyweds' foreheads were dripping with sweat in the now scorching sun. They then posed, just as Melanie and Dirk had done back then, to record their wedding vows on this breathtaking beach.

Melanie and Dirk congratulated the newlyweds. The girls and Dirk put on their snorkelling gear and jumped into the water. Melanie remained lying on the blanket and felt a slight tingling in her stomach. Maybe she would meet her grandmother tomorrow.

They drove home in the afternoon satisfied, but they still had some work to do. Melanie phoned Kaleo to make sure he had everything ready for the competition.

"You don't have a band," the children heard Melanie say a little louder into the receiver of her cell phone.

"A music system is good, too," she then replied and hung up.

The family went to bed early because the first heat was already scheduled for 9 o'clock.

SURFING COMPETITION

The next morning, the family got up very early. Leilani and Lanea were excited. Leilani felt a bit of a stomach ache, which often occurred before her gymnastics competitions. Lanea, on the other hand, only seemed a little nervous as she could hardly eat anything at breakfast.

Melanie braided two braids for each of her girls. She then hugged them tightly and spoke to them, "Listen to me! Don't worry so much. Just have fun out there." Then, she whispered to them as she did every morning: "Dear God—"

"Protect me," they answered her.

"Which surfboard should we take?" they asked at the same time.

"Take a look at the waves and decide for yourself. I can't make that decision for you."

Dirk stood there and applied a little pressure by tapping his wristwatch. They both looked out of the large panoramic window and studied the waves. They walked into the garage and decided on their fishboards.

"If you take a closer look at the tail, the back of the surfboard is shaped like a fish fin! With their flatter rocker and wider outline, they are super-fast when surfing down the line. Speed is their big advantage for mastering tricky sections and creating the basis for more vertical turns. Good decision," she said to her girls.

Melanie opened the surf school at 8 a.m. Dirk helped her set up the seating and surfboards on the beach. Kaleo was already there and set up the awning for the competition judges and a small stage made of wooden pallets with a music system on top. The beach bar owner also set up his tables, chairs, and umbrellas. The girls warmed up and ran a few laps of the beach. Mr Reves joined the rest of the students and helped set up. The beach slowly filled up. The twin sisters ran into the arms of Leilani and Lanea. Melanie checked the surf conditions on her app. The wave period was ten seconds. The wave height had been set at 1.6 metres for the morning.

"Great conditions! Not too small and not too big."

Someone tapped her on the shoulder. When she turned around, she saw Katy's beaming face, carrying the flag folded over her arm.

"You actually made it," Melanie hugged her, a little bit bemused.

Katy smiled proudly from ear to ear.

"Please bring them to Kaleo. He should put them up now, please."

Katy nodded understandingly at Melanie and went off. Melanie watched the two of them out of the corner of her eye as she sorted the lyra shirts by size.

They fit together very well, she mused with a grin.

Kaleo threaded the flag, took a deep breath, and slowly pulled it up step by step. The flag waved in the wind and had a unique print. Katy had chosen dark blue lettering and decorated it with three large, colourful plumeria flowers. Melanie knew why she had chosen three. Three is the number of *happiness and success*. We distinguish between the trinity of heaven, earth, and hell and know the divine Trinity: Father, Son, and the Holy Spirit. Knocking on wood three times brings good luck.

Melanie was very pleased with the flag. Satisfied with Katy's design, she sought the brief attention of her girls. She spotted them among the spectators and caught a smile from them because of the flag. Satisfied, she stepped up to the referee's desk, where Kaleo and four judges had already gathered. Melanie greeted them with a friendly Aloha and thanked them for coming.

Kaleo was given the role of speaker. He was to comment on the surfing competition and provide the spectators with all the information they needed. Kua, Kaleo's friend from the Big Island, took on the role of beach marshal. He checked the participants and was to hand over the competition lycra shirts.

"Who's our lifeguard?" asked the surf instructor, Mr Reves, as he joined them.

"Good question." They hadn't even considered that.

"Excellent, then I'll gladly take on the role," Mr Reves said.

Melanie was very grateful to him, but suddenly everyone was looking out to sea. "Who's that in the water?" she wanted to know.

An elderly surfer paddled out with his surfboard, sat resolutely lined up in the surf, and studied the waves.

"That's Kanaloa out there," Kaleo explained to them.

She remembered the god of the ocean and the winds. She was extremely impressed by his appearance and posture. His arms were also completely tattooed.

Melanie and the rest couldn't believe their eyes as he paddled in briefly and rode his oceanic wave like a majestic god. In the end, he kicked himself off the board with a kick out like a king and jumped into the breaking wave like a dolphin.

"He's just checking the conditions; he's the Dawn Patrol," Kaleo told her in passing.

Melanie felt a little silly as she studied the conditions in her wave app. The Hawaiian god of the ocean and winds came out of the water and was taken in by the twin sisters. They hugged, talked, and danced on the shore of the beach. The twin sisters pointed at Melanie, and he sought her attention, waving a hang-loose at her in a friendly manner. Melanie turned bright red and waved back.

He introduced himself at the referee's desk, "I'm Kanaloa, the great-uncle of the twin sisters. I've heard a lot about you. You have cute girls." He had a lot in common with the surf instructor from Biscay. "Mahalo, that the girls were allowed to stay with you."

"No need to thank us," she said quietly.

"We start in 30 minutes," said Kaleo and thanked the spectators for coming through the speakers.

"Can I store my sacred surfboard in the surf school for a while? I'd hate to leave it out here."

"Of course." She went with him to the surf school and showed him a safe place to park.

"They say you're half Hawaiian! Do you have family in Hawaii?"

Then she heard her name being called. It was her husband. *You could always count on him*, she thought sharply. "Honey, we're here."

Dirk came running towards her and looked stressed.

"Honey, we're missing the pineapples."

She remembered that the supplier could only deliver between 9 and 10 a.m.

"The pineapples will be delivered by 10 a.m.," she quickly reassured him.

"Honey, this is Kanaloa from Kauai, the great-uncle of Kiana and Kalea."

Dirk took a quick look at his tattoos and shook his hand.

"Family tradition," Kanaloa answered his curiosity, but Dirk still looked intrusively at his tattoos.

Melanie was super uncomfortable.

"They have a long tradition. They symbolise Hawaiian legends and are mysterious," explained Kanaloa to Dirk succinctly.

"Great kick out just now. Your brother, Koa, is already here with his wife, Kehaulani."

"I know; I've already welcomed the twins."

"Later, I will also introduce you to my family. My wife, our grandchildren, and my mother are on landing."

"We're looking forward to it," they assured him.

Dirk and Kanaloa went out together.

I hope Dirk doesn't say too much, she hoped. Even though he had just saved her life again. *Oh God, how exhausting my secrecy is.*

I'm getting to know my grandmother. And the girls will meet their great-grandmother, were her thoughts.

She couldn't describe how happy she was. She had never seen a picture of her. She had only seen a few pictures of her father. The speakers sounded outside.

Kaleo asked all participants to step up to the judges' table. When she came out of the surf school, the participants had formed an exemplary queue. Melanie joined the judges. She had already divided up the heats and handed them over to the judges. They checked the participants' names and gave them their lycra shirts.

Each school had its own colour. The students from Lanea and Leilani's school wore pink lycra. The pupils from the west of the island were given bright green lycra shirts. The pupils from the far east of the island were given yellow shirts.

Kiana, Leilani, Kalea, and Lanea now approached the table and grinned brightly and respectfully into Kanaloa's eyes. "Come on, I want a picture with you." Kanaloa stood up and joined the girls.

They formed the 'hang loose' sign with their hands, and Melanie proudly photographed them with her cellphone.

"I'll give you one more tip, girls," Melanie reminded them, leaning in front of them. "When the sets roll in, don't take the first wave because then you run the risk of being overrun by the following ones and barely have time to paddle back to the line-up quickly. Take your time; study the waves when you're out there on your surfboards. There are currently 1.5 minutes between sets. If you don't ride a wave in a set, expect a new set after 1.5 minutes—as of now."

Motivated, the girls continued to warm up. The time had come. Kaleo called out the participants of the first heat. He called out Lanea's and the other two girls' names. Lanea looked at Melanie expectantly. With her two plaited braids and pink Lycra shirt, she looked like a surfing competitor who wanted to prove her passion to the audience.

"Go on, my darling, you can do it." Melanie tied the leash around her ankle.

Lanea clamped her fishboard under her arm and marched towards the sea. The other competitors followed her. Lanea stood still while the other two continued on, fighting their way back through the sets.

When the set rolled out, she paddled leisurely towards them. She was less exhausted than her competitors.

A shrill, loud sound rang out, signalling to those battling on the sea that the clock was now ticking. Melanie looked around, and the beach was filled with spectators. She had never seen it so full before. She thought of her daughter, Lanea, and crossed her fingers tightly. There was pure excitement and thrills. They gazed expectantly at the glittering sea in its most incredible colours. Two minutes had already passed, and no one was paddling off. Lanea lay on her surfboard and looked behind her. Her eyes were fixed on a new set of rolling waves. Her opponents paddled off. One rode the wave to the shore, and the other fell into his breaking wave. Another two minutes passed, and Lanea was still lying on her board.

"Oh dear, she must be excited. Take your time, but not too long," said Melanie.

The next set of waves rolled in. She paddled off slowly and took on the third wave of the set. She increased her paddling speed considerably with her little arms. She recognised the peak, the highest point of the wave, and paddled even harder to pick up speed.

Kanaloa briefly looked up at Melanie and Dirk and smiled at them with an approving gesture.

"Tuberide," Kaleo announced through the loudspeakers.

The wave broke hollowly, forming a tunnel of water. Crouching, Lanea surfed through her barrel like a celestial being. She put her hands on her surfboard, glided to the end of the wave, and jumped happily into the water. She surfaced and waved to her parents. The spectators cheered and clapped loudly.

Kaleo announced over the loudspeakers that Lanea was currently in the lead. The other two sat in the surf and surfed more waves. Lanea sat in the lineup on her surfboard, dangling her legs in the water and looking up at the open sea. Kaleo announced the last two minutes through the speakers. Lanea lay back on her surfboard and paddled off. The wave pushed her forward. She stood up and rode a slightly smaller wave. She was at the highest point of the wave again and decided to do a floater. She kept her upper body parallel to the board, stretched her legs, and held her hands behind her back. Shortly after standing up, she turned her surfboard sideways towards the edge of the wave.

"Floater," Kaleo shouted through the speakers.

Lanea tried to extend the wave using her speed. So, she took advantage of the foam of the breaking wave. This meant great balance, as the fins under the surfboard didn't find a good grip in the foam of the wave. It was a daring manoeuvre. But Lanea held on until the end. She paddled out again. The other two were just paddling off again.

"Two waves aren't enough!" Lanea's mind flashed. She aimed for the highest peak of the incoming wave, paddled short and hard, stood up, let herself be carried away by it, and kicked herself on the wave crest upwards from her surfboard. She spun in the air and dropped appropriately into the water. 'A kickout' sounded through the speakers. Two loud signals sounded one after the other. The heat was over.

Kanaloa looked at Melanie in amazement. "You've only been here a few weeks!" She laughed in the face of the god of the ocean.

"You can also learn to surf outside of Hawaii."

Kanaloa was thoroughly impressed with her. As the competitors of the first heat stood at the judges' table, Kanaloa announced that Lanea had the most points and had, therefore, qualified for the third round. For the other two, there was still the second round, the so-called hope heat. In the second round, the heats were held one-against-one as an elimination competition. The better of the two surfers reached the next round; the other had to bow out. Leilani hugged her little Kamikaze sister and proudly congratulated her.

"Lanea, that was really great," they heard an older, unfamiliar, and gentle voice say. They turned around and looked at a small, petite old lady with long, thick, gray, loose hair and dark brown, almond-shaped, very bright eyes. Her face was tanned, narrow, wrinkled, and had the same noticeable birthmark that Melanie had. She wore an elegant red robe with enchanting Hawaiian embroidery. Overall, this woman looked like a real native Hawaiian.

Kanaloa greeted the lady with a long, tentative hug. "Aloha, Mama!"

Melanie's breath caught in her throat. There she was, her grandmother. Melanie could feel her energy, which she exuded, becoming increasingly weaker. Her legs became like pudding. She was paralszed.

"This is Melanie and Dirk with their girls from Germany. She's half Hawaiian," Kanaloa told her.

She looked at Melanie in a way she had never experienced before. She looked deep into her eyes, briefly examined the birthmark on her cheek, took a step back and focused on her overall appearance.

"I am Haumea Binkom," she said and held out her hand to the paralysed Melanie.

The goddess of fertility, it flashed through Melanie's head, awakening her from her paralysis. She gently shook her bony yet soft-feeling hand.

Kaleo called the participants of the next heat. After two more heats, Leilani was finally called.

Haumea Binkom looked for a shady spot at the beach bar.

Leilani got ready and looked at her mom.

"You'll manage; you're experienced. Concentrate, you can read the waves."

Leilani took another quick drink of water and set off.

In the meantime, Melanie got the judges something to drink. Dirk and Melanie met briefly at the beach bar, and he whispered to her, "How are you? Your grandmother seems very nice."

I feel good in her presence, she thought. But she didn't have time to let her thoughts run free. She had to devote all her concentration to the competition.

Dirk happily received the pineapple delivery man. Together with the other competitors, they sat line-up in the water.

The start signal sounded. Leilani paddled off too slowly, and the oncoming set rolled on without her. She looked nervous. She paddled and set off with much more determination and power this time. She felt the thrust of the wave piling up behind her and jumped onto her surfboard like a heavenly child. She felt the impulse of the wave's descent, slid down a little with her surfboard, and immediately initiated a turn to escape the breaking part of the wave and surfed along the wave's face.

"Bottom turn," sounded from the loudspeakers.

The spectators applauded her loudly. As the waves rolled on, she pulled her surfboard back by the leash and paddled off again. It bothered her that her sister could surf a tube. She wanted to, too. She paddled to the spot where she thought the highest point of the wave might be. She paddled more powerfully, and the wave pushed her slightly. As she stood on her surfboard, the wave broke hollow at the point, and she also surfed a tube in a crouched position. She looked breathtaking.

The final signal of the heat sounded. A short time later, Leilani and the other competitors curiously approached the referee's desk. The judges were conspicuously arguing with each other. Kaleo announced to the spectators that Leilani had taken the lead and manoeuvred herself into the third round.

Lanea hugged her older sister. "I didn't know you were so good at that manoeuvre," she teased her.

Kiana and Kalea were now getting nervous, too, because they would soon be called up. Haumea took her great-great-granddaughters to the side. She calmed them down and told them an old story from times gone by. Leilani and Lanea sat down curiously.

"Mana, all power comes from within. The power to change one's own life does not lie with a higher authority, like parents, God, boss, or government, but with yourself. You are (at least partly) responsible for everything that happens to you in life."

After a few more heats, Kaleo called up Kiana. Only now did Melanie notice Kanaloa's wife. She was sitting far away with her two little granddaughters on a turquoise-coloured beach blanket next to the surf school. Melanie estimated the children to be between three and five years old.

Kiana had great posture and surfed several waves with confidence. So did the other competitors.

It's a good thing I don't have to award points, she thought with relief.

When the heat was over, it turned out that Kiana had also narrowly made it to the third round. Kaleo announced a 30-minute break. Kanaloa got up and went to his wife and grandchildren. Dirk had provided Haumea and the girls with a drink and a hot dog. Kehaulani and Koa sat with her. Koa looked a little angry, and Kehaulani tried to calm him down. When Kanaloa joined them with his wife and grandchildren, Koa calmed down again.

"I wonder what the conversation is about?" Melanie asked curiously. "But it's not really any of my business."

The beach bar filled up with hungry spectators. Dirk and the owner had plenty to do. Kaleo played soothing Hawaiian music in the background. The atmosphere was enchanting. Melanie took some time out and, with a hot dog in her hand, went back into the air-conditioned surf school to enjoy the peace and coolness. As she sat at her desk in the anteroom and was about to take a bite of her hot dog, Haumea Binkom entered her surf school.

"Is it possible to freshen up here?" she smiled questioningly at Melanie. Melanie jumped up, showed her the way, and left her hot dog on her table. She waited patiently for Haumea in the anteroom of the surf school, craving her hot dog, which was probably already cold.

"How long have you lived here on Maui?" Haumea wanted to know, approaching Melanie expectantly and holding her antique cane in her right hand.

"We moved here exactly three weeks ago."

Haumea looked at Melanie again. "What's your father's name?" she suddenly asked her directly.

Melanie didn't know what hit her and looked at her speechlessly. "His name is..." she tried to answer but couldn't get over her shadow, so she remained silent and stared at the ceiling. She fought back tears. When she regained her composure, she looked Haumea straight in the face. "I don't want to name him."

"You don't have to, Melanie." The way she emphasised the name Melanie sounded scary to her ears. But Haumea smiled cheerfully at Melanie, took her right hand, and stroked it for a while. Neither of them said anything. Haumea's gaze penetrated deep into Melanie. She broke away from her and walked out again in silence.

Melanie was ashamed; she was never disrespectful, especially to older people, but she just couldn't bring herself to do it. She ran into the changing rooms and cried from the bottom of her heart. Huddled together, she let her tears run free.

It's a good thing nobody has to change, she thought as she looked in the mirror. Her eyes were all red. Even her waterproof mascara couldn't withstand her tears. She quickly fetched her sunglasses and put them on. That way, no one would see her eyes.

I can't do this; I have to get out of here, pounded in her head. She took her favourite surfboard under her arm, tied the leash around her ankle, and headed straight for the ocean. She needed the ocean now more than ever.

No other place in the world made her feel better. She stuck her sunglasses in the sand and ran into the water. She sat line-up in the surf. Her gaze was directed towards the open sea for a long time.

She enjoyed the dance of the waves beneath her surfboard, which rocked her gently back and forth. She thought of her mother, who had never said a word to her about her Hawaiian family. About her gorgeous, good-looking grandmother, her uncle and their children. Like Pelé, the fire and volcano goddess, she was about to erupt again.

As this was nothing like her, she calmed down. She lay back on her surfboard, gazed up into the blue sky and enjoyed the rocking. "Mana," she had learned from her grandmother, "you are responsible for everything you do."

She knows exactly who I am! she reminded herself and felt incredibly uncomfortable.

"Mana," she sang softly. Determined, she rolled from her back to the stomach position and fell off the board. *How embarrassing!* she thought and got back on her surfboard.

As usual, she looked over her right shoulder at the approaching waves. Gliding, she held her right hand just above the surface of the water. She recognised the highest peak right away and slowly began to paddle. She positioned herself at the highest peak of the incoming wave, paddled quickly, and—while it pushed her—she hopped onto her board like a real chief's daughter. She bent her knees and surfed the most unbelievable wave of her life, making herself as small as possible to surf through the tube.

Kaleo's voice sounded from the loudspeakers. But she didn't understand what he was saying. When she had ridden the wonderful wave to the end and absorbed the energy of the wave, she dropped onto the board and paddled slowly back to the shore. Kanaloa was already waiting for her there. He held out his hand to her.

"You remind me of my mom out there."

Melanie was surprised and took his hand. He pulled her out of the water with a powerful tug. Embarrassed, she looked past him and kept an eye out for her girls among all the spectators.

With renewed courage, she made her way to the beach bar. Dirk placed a cool drink in front of her and beamed at her. But he quickly realised what she looked like.

"I'll tell you later," she whispered to him. She looked for her grandmother, who was happily playing with her great-grandchildren just two tables away.

How elegant and sprightly this woman was. The spectators returned to their seats as Kaleo announced the next heat. It was Kalea's turn. She simply rode as many waves as she could. She didn't do any manoeuvres like Leilani or Lanea did. But neither did her opponents.

"That's a point deduction," Kanaloa said sadly to the crowd.

When the heat was over, Kalea came to the referee's table, upset. "Uncle, I was too excited. I don't want to compete again."

Kanaloa looked at her urgently.

"Excuse me, young lady? A Hawaiian Binkom doesn't give up that easily. You speak well with your world champion title. And Uncle Kāne. You just need more experience in competitions and more training. It's your first one. You're doing pretty well for that," he encouraged her.

Kalea hugged her great-uncle and sat down next to her great-grandmother. They watched the other participants for a while. It was a great atmosphere; a light breeze was blowing, the sky was bright blue, and the spectators were in high spirits. Music played in the background, and Melanie was composed again.

My father was once a world champion, too? she thought. *What else am I supposed to endure today?*

Dirk took her aside when the next big break was announced. "Come on, honey, let's go for a walk. I need a break."

They strolled along the crowded beach to her terrace. There, she told him about her encounter with her grandmother at surf school.

"She knows," Dirk gushed.

Melanie looked at him with completely dazed eyes.

"We have to get back. The kids are competing for the quarter-finals."

They had already spent time in the blazing sun since the start of the competition. They ran off in the direction of the surf school. Out of breath, they arrived in good time because Kaleo called Lanea for the quarter-final competition. Lanea was already ready; she was standing in front of the ocean with her surfboard and was just about to set off when Melanie pulled her back by her pink lycra shirt.

"I love you, my darling, no matter how this turns out. You're my winner."

Lanea gave Melanie a big kiss on the cheek and paddled out to the others. Line up, the two wished each other good luck. The swell had become wilder and higher.

They heard the start signal. Her opponent reared up like a bull and then fell into the breaking wave. Lanea, athletic and skillful, slid down the wave from the peak out along the wave face.

"Wonderful!" exclaimed Kaleo.

They sat line-up again. Lanea was just standing on the wave when the competitor dropped in. He simply drove into her. They both collided and fell into the water.

"Disqualified," it sounded from the speakers.

Her competitor had taken her wave. That was a quick end in Lanea's favour. Now, Leilani and her competitor were called. Leilani was always very sensitive and took everything to heart as a result. Excited, she took her board and gave Dirk another kiss. Melanie accompanied her belly-deep into the water.

"You can do it, my darling," she told her.

The waves were higher than ever. They weren't used to such heights very often. On the beach, her app showed 1.90 metres. If she fell into the water, she would be swept over by heavy waves. She paddled out gracefully like a queen. Melanie loved watching her paddle. Nothing disturbed her now. She sat there and looked around. The signal sounded.

Her competitor took the first wave of the set, fell, and was rolled over by the following waves. Leilani lay down on her board and looked over her shoulder to the left. She studied the waves and set her sights on the fifth wave of the new set rolling in. She lifted the surfboard over the wave and rode it with just the back part of the surfboard.

"Roller!" shouted Kaleo.

The audience literally exploded. A huge applause rang out. So she was also in the quarter-finals. Leilani stepped up to the judges' podium.

Kanaloa looked at her. "The maneuver is difficult; how did you do it?"

Leilani laughed briefly and answered him:

"I have the best surf instructor in the world," she said, looking at Melanie.

Melanie hugged her close to her. It was already late in the afternoon, but the spectators stood their ground.

Mr Reves approached the competition table. "The Ocean Sisters that win the competition!"

"Ocean Sisters?"

"They're unpredictable out there."

Kanaloa laughed and asked the girls to come a little closer.

"Have you noticed that the waves are getting higher and higher?"

Everyone looked out to sea and nodded.

"Can you do it?"

They laughed.

"Then it's fine; I didn't say anything," he said and leaned back in his chair again.

Lanea scrutinised her competitor. The girl was blonde, slim, and very tall for her age. Lanea made jokes with her as they paddled out together. The start signal sounded and they both sat line-up.

Who would surf the most points? The spectators, Haumea, Melanie, and Dirk, stood with their feet in the water. Another wave set rolled in, and Lanea was always confident enough to go first. She took on the sixth wave of the set. She quickly reached the peak and shot out of the tube in a crouched position. She held her arms calmly outstretched. But her competitor didn't move. She sat there and let the dreamlike waves roll past beneath her. Lanea paddled towards her.

"What's wrong?"

The girl looked at her, crying. "The waves are too high for me; I don't dare."

The fear was written all over her face, Lanea realised. She thought about it for a moment.

"I'll help you, but why are you paddling out here in the first place?"

"I didn't want to let down my parents and siblings." She held onto the back of her surfboard.

"Okay, then just stay on the board until the end. Don't get up and hold on tight," she emphasised.

The wave came and pushed her. Unlike usual, she slowed her board down a little and only let go when the wave started to break. In this way, she took the speed away and was able to rush down the wave lying down. It was clear that Lanea had qualified for the final.

On the beach, the girl's parents thanked her. Kanaloa congratulated her. Lanea had now made it to the final, but for Leilani, the decision was still to come.

Leilani warmed herself up. When it was her turn, she entered the water, and Dirk accompanied her knee-deep. She sat in the surf with her competitor from the neighbouring school. The two of them got on well and chatted. The starting signal sounded. Leilani immediately lay down on the board while her competitor was still sitting on the board. Melanie could see that she was studying the waves rolling in from so far out in the Pacific. Melanie held her breath. She paddled with long strokes to the peak; the wave broke, and she shot through the tube. The wave was so big that she didn't even have to crouch down. The spectators applauded loudly with enthusiasm. Unfortunately, her fellow competitor had not been able to perform such great maneuvers. When Leilani stepped out of the water, she was pushed back into the water by her friends. Lanea and her friends hugged her underwater. So, they were both in the finals.

Unfortunately, Kiana and Kalea and James and Jones only made it to the quarter-finals. Melanie asked her girls to come to the surf school for a moment.

"You know, I'm incredibly proud of you! Which manoeuvre do you want to perform? With the right one, you'll walk out of here as winners today."

"Roundhouse cutback!" shouted the girls at the same time. Melanie put a surfboard on the floor and imitated again what they had to do to perform it.

"And if it doesn't succeed?"

"Why wouldn't it?!"

"The wave is high enough; you can even do it two or three times in the wave. Keep your arms wide while you're turning. See, like this," and she turned 180 degrees on the surfboard.

The girls looked at each other mischievously. Suddenly, Haumea came in.

"Roundhouse cutback! I wish you good luck, girls!"

The girls thanked her and went out. They sat down on the shore and watched the other heats in progress.

The finalists had now been decided. Lanea was called up. Her fellow competitor was built similarly to her. The only thing that made them different was their hair and the colour of their lycra shirts. They both took their surfboards and went out. The wave height dropped to 1.6 metres at twelve seconds. The start signal sounded.

Melanie was excited and didn't want to look. She held on to Dirk. Lanea's fellow competitor took the third wave and surfed a beautiful tube to the end. She herself paddled up to the highest peak at tremendous speed, shot along the wave face, turned 180 degrees just before the foamy part, and surfed along to the other side of the wave wall. Due to her speed, she was able to turn 180 degrees again and surfed until the wave wall collapsed, and then she jumped into the water with a kickout. The spectators, as well as the Binkom family and her family, were speechless.

"Roundhouse cutback!" shouted Kaleo.

Both paddled line-up once more. They only had time to ride one more wave, and they paddled off.

From the beach, Melanie thought that a crash would follow, but Lanea's fellow competitor didn't get the wave. Lanea even managed to ride three cutbacks within one wave. The waves were predestined for this. The signal sounded.

"Such a little girl, how can she?" Melanie heard Haumea say.

"Our Year 5 winner is Lanea!" they heard Kaleo shout through the loudspeakers.

Her teammate congratulated her. Lanea came running up to Melanie, and she lifted her into the air.

"Mom, how was my cutback?"

"Wonderful. I knew you could do that, my darling."

"The sixth-year finalists, please get ready."

"Now it's my turn," said Leilani.

Her companion was a head taller but built just like her. She had a blond mop of hair and had moved here from North America.

They both paddled out quickly. They waited in line-up for the perfect wave. Leilani began to read the waves.

Suddenly, they paddled out at the same time, but Leilani knew that if she reached the peak faster, her fellow competitor would be out. She managed to reach the peak first. The wave pushed her on but rolled on without her. Unsettled, she searched for her companion, who had taken the wave after her, as she was unable to find her for a short time. Another set of waves rolled in. She paddled off, jumped on, and rushed along the wall of waves. Just before the foaming part of the wave, she turned her surfboard with a jerky movement and rode along the other side. The wave broke, and she kicked herself upwards into the water. She surfaced, grabbed her board, and paddled off again.

She was wondering how many minutes she had left when she saw that her competitor was surfing a tube. The next wave came and pushed her forward. She hadn't done this often before, but she wanted to give it a try. On the crest of the wave, she turned 360 degrees with her surfboard and finally fell into the breaking wave. A few seconds passed, and the surfboard was knocked back and forth by the waves, but she didn't surface.

Just as Melanie, Mr Reves, and other spectators were about to run into the water, she surfaced.

Melanie ran towards her. "What happened?"

"I don't know—the waves didn't let me surface."

Melanie was grateful that she was okay.

The judges argued wildly with each other as they stepped back to the podium. They were calculating the points of the best two waves. It was a close game.

Lanea stepped up to Leilani and whispered, "You'll be first, I'm sure. You did the 360-degree shoot," she envied her.

Melanie saw Kaleo take the microphone. "Leilani is the winner of Year 6!"

The audience freaked out with joy.

Leilani hugged Melanie tightly. "Mahalo, Mom!"

"What are you thanking me for? You did that on your own," Melanie responded, finally having tears of joy running down her face.

Dirk was watching everything from the beach bar.

He was incredibly proud of his girls.

Kanaloa approached the two of them. "I'm thrilled with your manoeuvres."

The girls were delighted and sat down at the Binkom family table. To the family they didn't know was their family.

"What a shame because it was on such special days that the family belonged together and should celebrate together," were Melanie's words of thanks.

When the last finalists were determined, the first-place winners lined up next to each other. The spectators, families, and friends took pictures of them.

Afterwards, they celebrated extensively and enjoyed themselves dancing on the beach. The twin sisters, Haumea, Kehaulani, Koa, and Kanaloa and his wife and great-grandchildren made their way to Lahaina. The restaurant was due to open.

"Are you coming with us?" Koa and Kehaulani asked Melanie and Dirk.

"We have to clean up here and would like to celebrate with our girls at home."

The families bid each other an understanding farewell. As the beach slowly emptied, Kaleo, the beach bar owner, Dirk, Katy, and the girls helped with the dismantling. Afterwards, they strolled home along the beach. The girls proudly told them their stories in a cosy atmosphere with an amazing view of the sunset.

KAUAI

The next morning, the children and Dirk were still in bed. The school was closed this Monday due to the surfing competition. Melanie wanted to get back into the ocean before she was going to teach. The weather literally invited her to do so. Just as she was about to go out, the doorbell rang.

So early in the morning, who will it be? Melanie wondered. When she opened the door, Haumea was standing in front of it with a nice smile. A red Wrangler was parked in front of the garage, but she was alone.

"Haumea, so early! Has something happened?"

"Quite a lot," she told her and entered without being asked. "I was just about to paddle out onto the ocean!"

"If I could do that, I'd love to." Melanie's big surfer heart began to bleed; how would she fare? All the conditions would be there to surf, but she would be too old for it. Unimaginable.

"Come on, let's go out together. I've got another softboard."

"I haven't done that in ten years."

"Then it's high time. I'll be careful, and we'll stay waist-deep."

Melanie dug out a light summer wetsuit. They were almost the same shape and size. Melanie helped her into the wetsuit. Slowly and bit by bit, Melanie pulled the wetsuit up on her like a second skin.

"I'm already completely exhausted by this thing."

Haumea laughed. Melanie knew that feeling only too well.

"The thicker the wetsuit, the harder it is to put on," Haumea pointed out.

They laughed together.

When Melanie pulled the zipper up to her neck, Haumea said tearfully, "Nice to have you here!"

Melanie froze for a moment. "I'm happy, too!" she replied.

They both walked carefully down the steps to the beach. Melanie knelt in the sand at their feet.

"Which leg is your stronger leg?"

"My right one."

"Mine, too," she answered and strapped the leash around her left ankle.

They entered the water together. The wave period was 20 seconds with a wave height of one metre. In the early morning, the waves were small at first, but by midday, they were getting bigger.

"Lie on it carefully; I'll push you slowly across the water."

As Haumea lay on the surfboard, she began to paddle out. Melanie could see how much she loved it. She was so happy that she almost started to cry. Melanie pushed her line-up while the small waves rolled into Haumea's face. She enjoyed being so in tune with the ocean. Melanie stood to the right of her soft board.

"Can you sit down?"

"I'm trying."

Wobbling, Haumea carefully straightened up.

"That I will experience this again. My children don't have time for that."

"That's why I'm here now."

They looked at the lush palm-fringed tropical forests in silence. They enjoyed the silence and the sound of the ocean.

"I love this view. I used to paddle out every morning like you. But when my son got sick and I took him in…" she fell silent. Melanie could see that she was fighting back tears.

"You mean Kāne?"

"Exactly, I cared for him for ten years. When he got weaker and weaker, and I couldn't do it anymore, we had him transported to Maui to his brother, Lono."

"Come on, let's ride a wave," Melanie said, and she looked at her with surfing passion.

"But I'm not getting up," Haumea laughed.

"Okay, then stay lying down. I'll nudge you."

A set of small waves rolled closer. Haumea paddled as best she could and slowly rode the wave to the shore lying down. Melanie swam to her and helped her up.

"Super good," she said and formed the 'hang loose' sign with her right hand. They both sat down in the sand.

Haumea looked at Melanie. "Where were you born?"

One minute, it was so idyllic, and the next, she didn't know what hit her. But then, she looked at her seriously.

"I was born in Texas."

Haumea looked at her with shining eyes and stroked her dark, wet hair dipped in salt water. "I thought I would never get to know you."

Melanie's tears rolled down her face. "I thought you wouldn't be alive," Melanie confessed.

"My son, Kāne, was the most difficult of all my sons," Haumea began. "I took him to the US Army so that he could become sensible. Tell me what he was like as a father?" she asked Melanie urgently.

Melanie got goosebumps. She stared at the sea and answered, "Self-confident and authoritative."

Haumea now stroked her shoulder. "That sounds a lot like Kāne. I don't know what I did wrong." She began to cry again.

Melanie comforted her, "'*We are all responsible for our own actions,* 'Mana, a wise woman, once said to me. I have forgiven him!"

Melanie went on, "It was fate that our girls became friends with your great-great-granddaughters. Then, Lono also introduced himself with his surname. After a while, it became clearer and clearer who my relatives were."

"I think we have a lot to talk about," said Haumea, jumping up as if she were 30 years old.

"The children don't know."

"I understand; take as long as you like. I want to show you something. Come with me to Kauai. Our flight leaves at noon today."

"Our flight?"

"Your family is invited, too."

"The surfing students are waiting for me."

"Nonsense, just close it for me today."

Melanie was looking forward to a trip and agreed. They happily went back into the house. The children and Dirk sat at the table and had breakfast.

"Would you like something, too? That looked great, by the way!" said Dirk.

Haumea smiled bashfully.

"In the past, it would have looked like your wife or your girls."

They had breakfast together and talked about the wind.

"The wind is the main cause of waves. When it blows across the sea, lake, or riverbank, small waves are created by friction. The stronger and longer the wind blows, and the larger the area over which it blows, the larger the waves become. However, waves can also be caused by other factors, such as currents or undersea earthquakes. So when you sit on the beach or line up and watch the waves, you should always be aware that they are not only caused by the wind but by several factors," Haumea explained more breathtakingly than Melanie had ever heard before. Haumea stood up and said goodbye to them. "I'll see you at the airport."

Dirk and the children suddenly looked confused.

That's right, Melanie hadn't told them about her last-minute trip. "We're flying to Kauai at noon today. Haumea wants to show us something. She insists on it."

Dirk couldn't hide his grin, and the girls got ready to go. Melanie cancelled her appointments for today and hung the board in front of the surf school.

"Let's fly to Kauai!" Melanie said to her family.

They packed their bags, and two hours later, they were all back at Gate 3 in Kahului. The girls were delighted.

Kanaloa finally introduced his wife, "This is Laka. She was named after the goddess of dance. She was worshipped by the islanders for her hula dance. Now, I worship her." He laughed so loudly that some travellers looked over at him.

Laka took a step towards Melanie and Dirk. "It's a pleasure to meet you. Congratulations again to your girls. They really were the best out there on the ocean."

Melanie and Dirk thanked them for the great compliment. The girls played with their grandchildren, Luana and Hilo. Dirk didn't seem anxious this time. The whole situation outweighed his fear of flying.

The Hawaiian Airlines plane was full. Due to the last-minute booking, everyone was seated apart. Two beautiful Hawaiian stewardesses in floral costumes accompanied them on the 50-minute flight. They flew over Molokai, Lanai, and Oahu. They could see the islands from the airplane windows. As soon as they were in the air, they were already landing again. At the airport in Lihue, which was in the east of Kauai, they were picked up by a bus with the name 'Binkom Pineapple Plantation' printed on it.

"Are we going to your pineapple plantation? How beautiful it looks here," Leilani remarked.

Haumea sat on the bus with them and turned to Leilani. "They don't call Kauai 'the garden island' for no reason." Haumea told them that she was born on the Big Island but moved to New York for work. "I met your great-grandfather in Central Park."

Melanie sat next to her and gave her a gentle nudge. Haumea corrected herself, "I met my husband in Central Park. Can you tell me where Central Park is?"

"Near Times Square!" Lanea shouted proudly.

"So, I went jogging every morning. My husband was there on business for Kona Coffee. One morning, he just came up to me and asked me if he could marry me. I turned him down. But he didn't give up. He went jogging with me every morning, even though he didn't like jogging. Then he managed to gain my trust, and we went out. We fell in love and had a long-distance relationship for a long time. When I visited him on Kauai, I stayed for good. His name is Ku."

Haumea took a short break and continued, "I never went back to New York. I fell in love with this island. I helped him set up his plantations."

"What plantations?" Lanea called out.

"We own pineapple, papaya, banana, and coffee plantations. It was a tough time with three sons."

They drove along the Kaumuali Highway to the pineapple plantation in Waimea. They got out and looked at plantations as far as the eye could see.

"Would you like to take a tour of the plantations?" Haumea asked them curiously.

Kanaloa and Laka took the children to a large one-storey cottage painted beige, which stood very impressively at the beginning of the plantation.

Haumea and the rest set off. She told them that the first pineapple factory in Honolulu had opened in Oahu in 1906. Hawaii suddenly became the world's No. 1 pineapple supplier. Today, the islands only produced 15 per cent of the world's harvest.

"The pineapple will always be associated with Hawaii. Here, you can see how they are grown, harvested, and processed. There are large, small, long, and red varieties. We also have baby pineapples," Haumea explained proudly.

"We want to see them!" the girls shouted.

"Of course!" She then asked an employee to show the girls the baby pineapples. "Every pineapple is picked by hand. So there's no machine that you can just drive over the pineapple fields."

"In Germany, I often ordered the expensive Kona coffee online and served it on special occasions," Melanie told her. "Do you have the Kona plantation on the Big Island?"

"That's right," said Haumea, "you know quite a lot. Kona coffee is one of the most expensive coffees in the world. On the west coast of the Big Island, most of the coffee is grown in the Kona area. Arabica coffee grows on the steep slopes of Mount Halili and the Mauna Loa volcano. Pineapples, macadamia nuts, and Kona coffee are the most popular and famous products. Hawaii has the best conditions, thanks to its year-round, permanently mild climate and excellent volcanic soil. There are bananas, mango, papaya, tobacco, and coconuts."

"Who takes care of the Kona plantation?" asked Dirk.

"Kanaloa takes care of everything. He hardly sees his family, but he can make a good living that way."

"On the Kona plantation, fresh coffee is constantly being brewed for tourists and poured from thermos flasks into small paper cups. We offer coffee in different varieties, qualities, and price ranges, espresso varieties and flavored coffee specialties with macadamia flavor and the like. We only have small plantations. Some sold their plantations to multimillionaires, who in turn built luxury hotels. As a result, pineapple cultivation declined. We wanted to keep our plantations in the family."

"Have you been made an offer?" Dirk asked curiously as a businessman. Melanie was embarrassed by his question and gently stepped on his foot.

"Yes, they did. Only Ku knows the amount. He would never have sold his plantations for any money in the world. It was a hard time, and many plantation owners went bankrupt. Pineapple cultivation requires patience because it usually takes two to three years for a bud to grow. But we have always managed to keep our heads above water."

After a while, the girls came running up to her, beaming. "Mom, we've brought you some pieces; they're so delicious." They gave them a bowl full of different pineapple varieties.

Melanie and Dirk were delighted with the sweet fruit. "This is the best pineapple I've ever eaten," said Dirk with his mouth full. The children pulled him by his arms over to the plantations.

"Tell me, what exactly did you do in Germany?" Haumea asked Melanie curiously. "I trained as an industrial clerk. For a long time, I supported Dirk in his company as a sales assistant. I was responsible for everything from order entry to logistics and customer communication. Later, I decided to work for a company that was more international. I had been able to acquire knowledge in all areas, so I was knowledgeable enough to start my own business, so I opened a care facility."

Haumea was visibly impressed. "Then you must know a thing or two about management."

Melanie nodded.

"We don't need to export our products as we have our customers on the islands. However, the large manufacturers, who sell their products at dumping prices, often throw a spanner in the works. And Kanaloa lacks the experience or the time. I can no longer travel around. I'm glad he kept his banana plantation on Kauai. The tourists love our plantations; the income helps us to keep the plantations going and pay good wages. But his children want nothing to do with the plantation. Lono has bought a restaurant on Maui, but he continues to look after his papaya plantation. Kāne helped Kanaloa a lot when he resigned from the army."

Suddenly, they saw an old, petite little man walking towards them with his walking frame.

"My darling husband. Come, let me introduce him to you. Look, this is Melanie from Germany. I met her yesterday on Maui, together with her girls and her husband."

He stepped closer to Melanie, so close that she could feel his breath, and greeted her with an *'Aloha.'* "Haumea's guests are also my guests. Do you like the plantation?" he said.

Melanie smiled at him because she knew it was her grandfather. "Pretty child. Haumea, when are we going to have our coffee?"

Haumea looked at her watch. "It's time for our coffee and banana bread. Come on, our staff know where we are and will bring your family right away."

They walked a little further through the plantation. In the middle of the plantation, Melanie spotted a small white colonial-style cottage. Melanie understood what Haumea meant: *New York against this was unbeatable*.

On the porch, they had a great view of the pineapple plantation, as far as the eye could see. Dirk and the girls joined them in a relaxed atmosphere.

"Have you been to Kauai before?" Haumea asked the children.

They shook their heads.

"Do you fancy a helicopter ride? You really must see Kauai from above."

Her husband stood up silently and carefully went into the house. After a short time, he returned to them. "You'll be picked up in ten minutes."

"Picked up by whom?" Melanie asked her grandparents politely.

"By Dole, our friend. He doesn't have any guests at the moment, so he's making his way to us. You must see Waimea Canyon and the Napali Coast from a bird's eye view." Haumea was delighted and clapped his hands.

"Wonderful. Let's go to the landing site."

At the landing site, they heard the loud noise of a helicopter. They looked up and saw a black helicopter above their heads with *'Dole'* printed on it. It became windy as it approached. When it landed in front of them, it got even louder, and the girls held their hair tight. The rotors caused their hair to swirl violently in the air. Dole got out of his helicopter and stood in a crouched position in front of the boarding stairs to the passenger compartment and waved them over. Melanie took Leilani by the hand, Dirk took Lanea by his hand, and they followed Haumea slowly to the helicopter. They took their seats in the helicopter.

Dirk sat next to Dole at the front and whispered to him, "I'm an anxious guest."

Dole looked at him and replied, "Nothing will happen to you today," and happily tapped him on his left thigh.

"Please fasten your seatbelts," they heard him say through the headphones.

"Here we go," said Haumea. "Now, you'll be amazed."

The helicopter slowly took off into the air until it had an overview of the whole of West Kauai. What they saw was a true natural wonder. They flew over the metre-high mountains and cliffs.

"Jurassic Park was filmed here," the family heard Dole's voice say through their headphones. The girls looked out of the helicopter windows with fascination and looked at them. "You see, there are many areas, valleys, and beaches here that are completely cut off from civilisation," Dole continued.

They flew along the famous rocky coast of Napali, very close to the cliffs. After a while, they heard Haumea say through the headphones, "Now comes the best part." Dole flew into a crater, which translates as being called 'rippling water.' They were surrounded by many cascading waterfalls over 1,000 metres high.

"Beautiful," the girls marvelled. Melanie never wanted to tell Haumea that she had already been on this flight with Dirk. They enjoyed it nonetheless. After an hour, they landed safely back at the Binkom pineapple plantation. Kanaloa was waiting for the travel enthusiasts. "Have you been pulling your strings again?" he laughed at his mother.

Haumea nodded happily at him.

"We've prepared food. Why don't you come and join us?" Dole turned off his helicopter and followed the cheerful group.

"Laka would like to organise a small barbecue today. Everyone is welcome."

The girls were delighted and ran off in the direction of Kanaloa's cottage.

"The last few days have been exhausting for me. I need to lie down. What time is your flight?" Haumea asked her granddaughter tiredly.

Melanie replied, "At 7 p.m."

"Then I'll come by before then. See you later," she told her and left with Dole.

Kanaloa told them about the Kona plantation on the Big Island. They met Luana and Hilo's parents on their porch.

"Come on, I'll introduce you to my son, Keko, and his wife, Hina."

Melanie estimated them to be in their mid-30s. In conversation on the porch, Melanie asked them why they didn't want to look after the plantations.

"It's very hard to find good employees; you're never sure if a storm will devastate the plantation, and competition on the islands is very high. Exporting is out of the question due to the high transportation costs. We have children; we need secure jobs," Keko replied.

"What do you do for a living?" Dirk asked curiously.

Keko replied, "I'm a hotel manager in a well-known hotel here on Kauai."

Hina laughed and said, "I am employed as a service employee at the same hotel."

"Great," said Dirk. "That's probably where you got to know each other."

Hina smiled. Melanie felt really happy, and so did her girls. But suddenly that feeling of self-doubt and shame rose up in her again, just like at the airport in Frankfurt. She had to tell her girls that they were all part of her family. Luana and Hilo, the twin sisters, Kiana and Kalea, with whom they had already become friends. But how was she supposed to do that? Then, Kanaloa took over the conversation and asked her if they had ever been to the Big Island. Melanie shook her head.

"Then it's high time I invited you to visit our Kona plantation. Just let me know if you're planning a trip to the Big Island."

Laka offered them a plate of deliciously prepared fish. So, they began to eat and told them about their homeland. They heard Dole's helicopter flying over their heads.

It was time for her to leave, too. The bus was already waiting, and Melanie was surprised because Haumea had not shown her face. She was probably fast asleep, and so she thought nothing of it. They said their goodbyes and drove to Lihue airport. The girls were tired and dozed off during the flight.

Melanie looked at Dirk and said, "I have to tell the girls."

Dirk smiled and seemed pleased with her decision. "Your family here will understand why you've put it off for so long. We had to get used to Hawaii first."

Melanie was pleased with his wise words.

At home, Melanie was talking to her girls as they were snuggled up in bed again. "And what do you think of Haumea, Kanaloa, and the rest of the family?"

Leilani replied, "I think they're all really nice, and I think it's cool that they have their own plantations."

"You know, kids..." Melanie thought about it and started talking slowly, "I told you that my father lives in Hawaii."

"Yes," said the children.

"I found out that the sick man in the wheelchair is my father."

The girls' eyes suddenly popped out from under the comforter. They sat up.

"What do you mean, Mama?" asked Lanea.

"Well, the man the twin sisters told us about, remember? He's my father."

The girls just looked at her in disbelief.

"Well, that makes Kiana and Kalea your great-cousins."

"How cool is that?" Lanea shouted into the room.

"Lono and Koa are your great-uncles."

"And what is Haumea to us then?"

"Your great-grandmother."

"Ah, that's why she said that on the bus," said Leilani.

"How did she know you were her granddaughter, Mom?" asked Lanea.

"I didn't ask her, but I think it was easy."

"I'm sure she heard about us when we took the twin sisters in for a few days. Lono will have told her that a family with a half-Hawaiian mother called Melanie is looking after them. And maybe she used the surfing competition to look at you."

"Yes, that could be," Melanie whispered. "I'd like to ask you not to say anything to the twin sisters yet. I have to think about the best way to tell them. Deal?"

"Deal," said her girls.

She hugged them tightly and kissed them, as she often did. "Good night!" said Melanie.

"*Aloha ahiahi*," said the girls.

Melanie was happy because they had been attending the Hawaiian language course for some time. Dirk sat on the porch and told Melanie that the pool had been finished. They lay down together on their seating lounge and fell asleep elated.

INVITATION

The next morning was quiet. The girls went to school, and Melanie gave surfing lessons for a few hours. Dirk had gone to Lahaina to buy some pool equipment. Melanie sat outside the surf school and thought about the best way to tell the whole family: *That she was the sick man's daughter? That she and her family were relatives?*

The sun was shining on her face, and she remembered that Leilani's birthday was in two weeks' time. There wouldn't be a more suitable occasion any time soon. She planned everything down to the smallest detail.

The girls and Dirk ran towards Melanie.

"Mom, everyone at school congratulated us today," thye told her and held their trophies under her nose. "Our trophies will have our names on them and will be placed in the sports display case in a week's time."

"Wow, girls," she said, "that's really great. You've earned it, too. I also have some news for you."

The girls looked at her curiously. "It's your birthday in two weeks, Leilani; it's a Saturday. We're inviting all our family and friends. And I'll tell them then."

The girls jumped for joy in the sand, and Dirk looked thrilled, too. Dirk repaired a few areas in the surf school while Melanie paddled out to sea with her girls.

As the three of them sat lined up on their surfboards, Lanea said, "I'm happy to be here, Mom. All the people are nice; the weather is always nice."

"Except for the storm," said Leilani.

"That's right, kids, together we're strong. Can you manage not to tell anyone anything for two weeks? I can imagine that it's not easy for you to do what I'm asking you to do."

"But, Mom, that's no problem for us. Look, there's a set coming; let's enjoy the freedom," they whined and paddled off.

At home, they designed beautiful, homemade invitation cards.

"Do we write the cards in Hawaiian?" the girls asked.

"If you can already do that. Then that's a great idea."

By the evening, they had finished making all the invitations. Happy with the decision to announce it on Leilani's birthday, the family went to bed.

The next morning, Melanie received a message from Kanaloa: '*Aloha, Melanie, our friend, Dole, passed away last night.*'

Melanie couldn't believe it.

She read on: '*He died of a heart attack. He was only in his mid-60s. We don't know what to do; the funeral is due to take place this week. We wanted to ask you if you could look after our children and the sick old man. I understand that you had a care facility in Germany.*'

Melanie was struck by lightning. Not because she was supposed to look after the twin sisters, but because she was supposed to look after her father. She spoke to Dirk, who was drinking his coffee by the pool.

He was also shocked about Dole's death.

"Poor man," said the girls as they sat down with their parents.

"What are we going to do now, children?"

Melanie asked the group.

"Watch out, Mom. And you'll see your father again after so many years."

Melanie had the urge to dash into the garage, grab her favourite surfboard, and paddle out mercilessly. But she didn't, she stayed put and replied: *'Dear Kanaloa, we're sorry to hear that. It really is very tragic. Of course, we'll watch them, just let us know when we should be there.'*

He replied with a *'Mahalo nui loa.'*

"Come on, kids, get ready for school," said Dirk.

"Here are the cards." Melanie gave him the invitation cards. They had decided that they should give them out today. When Dirk and the children were no longer to be seen, she sat out on the porch and watched the dancing, glittering, rolling waves that had already been on a long journey.

They wouldn't have as much to talk about as I did, she thought. Why did it all happen so suddenly? Was it fate? She thought of her favorite Catholic priest, Father Francis from Germany. He was of Indian origin and took exemplary care of his community. Melanie had enormous respect for his profession. After all, he had chosen to serve God. He always stood by his community in times of grief and need. His strength was definitely in always showing people that they were okay, no matter what situation they were in. He gave people courage and hope. Melanie really admired him for that. He would certainly also advise her to help the family. After all, there could be no confrontation with her father. He certainly wouldn't even recognise her, given everything she knew about his condition. She got ready for surf school and pursued her passion. Surfing—giving people the freedom they might long for.

The three tourists from Germany, who had registered via her website, were already waiting at the surf school. They greeted Melanie with an '*Aloha*' and not-so-good English. "We can also speak German." The tourists laughed in surprise.

"A Hawaiian who speaks German?" said one of the tourists.

Melanie corrected her, "I'm half-Hawaiian. My mother is German."

Oh dear, she remembered that she hadn't made contact with her since the last message. She wanted to make up for that later. She showed the tourists the dry runs in the sand. First paddling, then standing up and preferably standing still. The tourists were just as overwhelmed as she was at the time. When they were out on the ocean, they all had a lot of fun together. She loved the look on their faces the first time they had skimmed a wave. It always reminded her of her first time surfing in Maspalomas. As the original surfers bid her an overjoyed farewell, Kaleo slowly came trotting along.

"What's wrong?" Melanie asked him.

"Oh, nothing."

"Come on, tell me."

"I'm so alone here. Katy's back in Oahu; she has to work."

"Well, why don't you fly to Oahu?"

"I don't know," he grumbled.

"She likes you a lot, I could feel that, Kaleo."

"And what's new with you?"

Melanie sat down in the sand, and Kaleo sat down next to her. "You know, Kaleo, it's Leilani's birthday in two weeks. We'd like to invite you and Katy. Your card is still at home; I didn't know we'd meet today."

"That sounds wonderful. But aren't you looking forward to it?" he looked at Melanie.

"Yes, that's not the only thing. I'll tell you now: the sick man, the twin sisters' uncle, is my father."

Kaleo looked at the ocean and then at Melanie. "I'm sorry about that."

"Sorry for what?" she asked. "Well, that your father is seriously ill."

Melanie looked at him in horror but paused. "You know, Kaleo, it doesn't affect me. I don't feel anything when I think about him. It's been too long. 32 years is a long time. The Binkom family don't know about their new addition to the family yet, I suppose."

Melanie laughed. "Apart from you and Haumea, no one else does."

"How did she react?"

"She found out for herself."

Kaleo said, "She's always been a wise woman."

"I'll tell the rest of the family on Leilani's birthday," Melanie said.

"That's a nice occasion. We accept the invitation."

Melanie received a message from Kanaloa: '*Aloha, Melanie, the funeral will take place in two days. We fly from Kahului at 7 in the morning.*'

"What is Kanaloa writing?" asked Kaleo. "Dole, an old friend with whom we flew over Kauai the day before yesterday, had a heart attack yesterday and died."

"Dole!" Kaleo jumped up. "He was my friend. We used to go deep-sea fishing together a lot. But when he started his own business as a pilot 20 years ago, we rarely saw each other anymore." Stunned, he looked at Melanie. "He left us too soon. Please ask Kanaloa where the funeral is being held."

"He wrote '*Anini Beach Park.*' At his favorite beach in the north."

"I could have thought of that myself."

"A water funeral," Melanie remarked.

"Yes, that's right. There's a special ceremony for the ashes to be given to the sea. In Dole's case, the urn is safely taken out to sea on a surfboard by family and friends. A priest says Hawaiian prayers. The relatives wear white or colourful clothing and place flower garlands in the water. It is not the death that is mourned, but the life that is celebrated with the deceased. I will also be present."

Melanie commented, "I think that's good. We will look after the twin sisters and the sick man."

Kaleo paused.

Melanie blinked at him. "Let's leave it at that," she said. "Come on, I'll give you our invitation card. No one else is registered for today. I'm closing the surf school for the day."

"And when is the funeral?" Leilani asked as she walked in the door. "Aloha, I'm looking forward to seeing you, too."

"Tell me," she nagged.

"In two days. There's a water funeral for him," Melanie responded.

The girls had seen a funeral like this before in a music video.

"Why are you home already?" Dirk asked her when she got back.

"I have nothing more to do today."

Dirk mentioned that he had handed out all the cards. "And everyone agreed and received them with joy. They asked me what you wanted, Leilani," he told her and looked at her questioningly.

As if shot from a pistol, Leilani said, "An e-foil surfboard."

Melanie's breath caught in her throat. "You want an electrically powered surfboard? No way!"

"Why not?" Dirk asked her cautiously.

"Well, because that's not my attitude."

"Honey," he reassured her, "we live in the 20th century. If you offer this, too, you might be able to appeal to the younger generation."

"Exactly!" Leilani shouted defiantly.

"It's all the rage," Lanea added.

"I'll think about it," said Melanie stroppily.

What nonsense, you couldn't replace sacred surfing with electric surfboards. But they're all right. Who knows, it might be fun to glide along the waves, she thought.

Melanie conjured up a hot meal for her family.

Spaghetti Bolognese, just like she had always cooked in Germany. The girls went outside; this time, they had arranged to meet James and Jones. Melanie and Dirk sat on the porch while the girls splashed around in the fresh pool with James and Jones. Melanie wondered what it would be like to see her father again. Her staff had shown her how sick people were mobilised in bed or placed in a wheelchair with a lift. She had also been shown how bedridden patients were washed and changed. She had already had to do this several times when staff were unavailable.

In the evening, the family sat together in the living room and watched TV.

"Tomorrow, Kiana and Kalea will sleep with us."

"Right, Dad will drive you to school in the morning. In the afternoon, he'll take you to the pizza spot and then pick me up in Lahaina."

The girls nodded in understanding.

The next morning, Melanie wrote a condolence card for Dole's family and gave it to the girls. "Give the card to Kiana and Kalea; tell them to give it to Lono."

She had a busy day at the surf school. The pupils also wanted to learn the roundhouse cutback. Mr Reves and Melanie went to great lengths to show the experienced children. In the afternoon, she finished up at the surf school and went home. Her family was already waiting for her at home. Her cell phone rang. It was Haumea, thanking her for the invitation. She also thanked her for supporting her sick son.

"I'm happy to do this, thank you for your trust," Melanie said to her. "And my condolences for Dole."

Haumea fell silent. "It's sad. I have fond memories of him. Such a sweet guy. He was always by our side. I'm looking forward to seeing you again on Leilani's birthday. What does she want?"

"You won't believe it."

"What?"

"An e-foil surfboard."

"Like one of those electric surfboards?"

"Yes, exactly."

She remained silent. "This is a different age. Let's see what we can do. The family could pitch in. Everyone's invited, as I understand it. I'll bring it up."

"You don't have to."

"Let me do it, child," she said and took her leave with a mahalo.

"So?" Leilani looked at her mother. "Am I getting one?"

"I don't know," she stroked her hair.

"Kiana and Kalea are coming soon."

"That's right, we're going shopping. We'll prepare a German meal for them. What should we cook?"

"I would like Dad's vegetable soup."

"Then that's how it will be, let's go shopping."

At the supermarket, they met the principal, Mr. Wilhelm. He was standing on the other side of the parking lot.

"Mrs. Stein, nice to meet you. I heard your girls were wonderful to look at at the contest," he called out to them.

Melanie nodded. Leilani nudged her.

"This is our principle, Mom."

Melanie waved over to him and looked down at Leilani.

"He wasn't there, was he?" Leilani wrinkled her nose.

"No, he was unable to come. He has a disabled son," she whispered. She was sorry to hear that. Melanie said goodbye with the words, "My girls are loving the school."

They marched through the supermarket and did their shopping. At home, they prepared the vegetable soup together. Hula music was playing in the background, and the girls were dancing a kind of hula that Melanie and Dirk had never seen before.

"What a great job you're doing," said Melanie. "Come on, Mom, we'll show you. We have hula lessons once a week."

"Why don't you tell me about it?"

"Mom, you're always busy with your surf school."

Could that be true? Hadn't she gone away to spend more time with her daughters? She didn't make a fuss of it and danced after them. Suddenly, the doorbell rang. Sure enough, it was the twin sisters. Lanea ran excitedly and opened the door.

"Come in, we're cooking for you right now."

The smell of potatoes, vegetable broth, and sausages wafted towards them.

"Mmhh, that smells delicious," said Koa and Kehaulani.

"Come and eat with us," Dirk asked them.

They sat at the table and were all delighted with the soup. "You have to give us the recipe," begged Kehaulani.

"I'd love to," said Dirk.

When they had finished, the girls went to their rooms to play.

Koa gave Melanie a rundown regarding the care of Kāne, "It would be great if you could wash him. A wash bowl with washcloths for his upper and lower body, as well as towels and his toothbrush, are on the shelf to the right of his bed, along with his clothes. The hoist is in the hallway. When you've strapped him into the wheelchair, you can take him out onto the porch. He likes to watch the sunrise at breakfast."

"I thought he couldn't see," she shot out like a pistol.

"He can't either; he has maybe 10 per cent vision according to the last eye examination. But he can feel the wind and the environment. Anyway, his cereal is in the fridge. At half past eleven, you can heat up a pureed vegetable and potato mash, which is also in the fridge, in our microwave and serve it to him. After that, he usually wants to sleep, so you can mobilise him back to bed. If necessary, see if he needs to be freshened up again. He is usually awake again at 3 p.m. and would like to eat his banana bread. You can also serve it to him again on the porch."

"I'll probably find it in the fridge, too," Melanie said with a smile.

"There are plenty of drinks available. At 7 p.m., just before he goes to bed, he'll get some more porridge. It would be great if you could get him ready for bed by then."

"Does he still get medical care?" asked Me lanie.

"Yes, he gets tablets crushed in his cereal and in his midday and evening porridge. You'll find the tablets on the table on the left when you come in. He also wears compression stockings, which you would have to put on and take off for him."

"He likes being read to," remarked Kiana, who was just sitting down. "The books are on the shelf on the right."

"When will you be back at the latest?"

"We land at 8 p.m. Unfortunately, the flights before that were already fully booked at such short notice."

"That's all right."

"Unfortunately, we have received a storm warning. But we haven't received any information yet. We are assuming that there will be strong winds."

"As strong as last time?" asked Lanea.

"We don't know that yet. Our plane leaves at 6 a.m. tomorrow morning. It's enough if you're there at 7 a.m."

"Do you want to fly despite the storm?" asked Kiana and Kalea.

"We'll try. Anyway, we really want to be at the funeral. We're flying west. The storm is moving hundreds of kilometres south across the Pacific. We shouldn't get much," said Koa.

"Can you really do it?" Kehaulani asked Melanie.

Melanie looked at her, "Of course, please don't worry."

"Here's the key. It's best to go in over the porch. When you get to the restaurant, you'll see a staircase. His room is to the left of the stairs."

"Then I have all the information now. Dirk will drive me tomorrow morning," she said and looked over at him.

Dirk grimaced, "So early, then we have to leave at 6:30 a.m."

"You'll get ready in that time," Melanie said to the children.

They nodded.

Koa and Kehaulani said goodbye with a *'Mahalo nui loa'* and left. The girls spent the whole evening telling the twin sisters about their best friends, Ylvi, Mili, and Lia. They had grown up with them because their parents had grown very fond of Melanie and Dirk.

It was time to go to bed. The whole family went to bed, except Melanie. She sat on the porch and wondered what she had gotten herself into. She was looking forward to being able to care for such a sick man but not to meeting her father. Surely her agreement to care for him had to do with the fact that he couldn't know who would be caring for him. She went to bed with the thought of caring for a sick man and only fell asleep late at night.

IN FLAMES

Melanie got up very tired the next morning.

Should I put on my nursing scrubs? she pondered. She had brought her red tunic with the word *'Aloha'* printed on it from Germany as a memento. She had already practised the aloha spirit towards her employees, patients, and business partners in Germany. Quite successfully. She decided to put it on because she wanted it to give her a sense of security.

As she drank her coffee, Dirk sat down sleepily next to her. "That you can do this after it's been so long."

She wrinkled her nose. "He's a sick man. Besides, I'm happy if I can help the family," she replied, a little short-tempered.

Dirk noticed her tension. "You always have to help everyone."

"Yes, I have to."

Melanie woke the girls up and asked them to get ready for school.

"Dad will bring you to me after school."

The girls jumped for joy.

It was still dark on the way to Lahaina. As they stood in the parking lot next to the restaurant at 7 a.m. on the dot, the sunrise announced itself in its most magnificent colours. They watched the red ball of fire glide slowly over the horizon. Melanie unlocked the door and switched on the light.

"The light won't come on," she whispered to Dirk.

"I'll have a look for Koa's generator. We used that when we were building the roof when we had no electricity," he told her and disappeared.

Melanie waited outside on the porch and continued to watch the sunrise.

What a great view from the restaurant, she admitted to herself. The famous Front Street became livelier by the minute. *The houses are 200 years old,* she thought.

"You have power again now. Should we tell Lono?" He proudly approached Melanie.

Melanie shook her head.

"Will I get by with that for the day? They must have a lot to cool," were her concerns.

"The generator is running, otherwise call me… Do you need my help?" he suddenly asked her with a look of concern that she had never seen in him before.

"I'll manage. Go and see the children. And you'll come and visit me this afternoon."

She gave him a little kiss, and he drove off. She looked after him and was very grateful that he was always by her side. As he drove around the corner, she noticed that she had left her cell phone on the kitchen table.

Crap, that wasn't professional of me, she thought.

Now she was standing in front of the door next to the stairs, just as Koa had told her. She took a deep breath, took the door handle in her hand, pressed it down, and slowly pushed the door open. As she entered, she called out loudly, "Good morning, Kāne," and felt for the light switch. In the glow of the light, she saw him lying in his sick bed.

His comforter was pulled up to his neck. As she stepped closer to the bed, she saw his short gray hair, which had once been jet black. She stroked his shoulder and whispered in his ear, "Get up, I've come to take care of you."

He slowly opened his dark brown eyes. But he didn't look at her, instead staring past her at the ceiling. When she followed his gaze, she froze. She saw five photos of her and her siblings hanging from the ceiling. Distraught, she searched for the care utensils. She hadn't expected this. He was still staring at the ceiling. She grabbed the wash bowl and fetched warm water from the restaurant kitchen.

"Concentrate," she told herself.

When she re-entered the room with the wash bowl, he looked at her and followed her every move. She stood to the right of his bed and opened the bars. Then she raised the bed to her waist height. She announced, as she had learned from her nursing staff, that she would now raise the headboard. Using the remote control, she slowly raised his upper body to a vertical position.

Now, he looked her in the eye. Melanie smiled at him. His cheeks were still marked with small, fine scars. She remembered them. She took the warm washcloth and began to wash his hands, face, and ears. Slowly and carefully, she removed his sweaty T-shirt. Due to the power cut, the room was not air-conditioned enough. The room itself was only furnished with a table and two shelves. He lay there with his naked upper body. She washed his neck, his arms, and his upper body. But he didn't have a single tattoo, unlike all his brothers. When she had dried him off, she slowly put a fresh shirt on him.

What now? she pondered as he followed her every move. She took the comforter off the bed to freshen him up down below and put on his compression stockings.

"Done, now we can have breakfast," she said to him cheerfully.

He moved his lips, indicating a *"Mahalo nui loa,"* and smiled at her.

Oh God, she had forgotten about his teeth and brushed them very carefully. She fetched the hoist from the hallway and placed the carrying mat under his body. She hooked on the straps. She then positioned the wheelchair. She hadn't done that for ages. With his 1.90 metres and well-fed body, she slowly drove him from the bed up over the edge of the bed into the wheelchair. When he was sitting in the wheelchair, she released the hooks and strapped him firmly to the wheelchair. She then clipped the footrests to the wheelchair and lifted his legs onto them. Well, that was harder than she had thought. Happy to have made it, she slowly drove him straight down the narrow corridor through the restaurant and out onto the porch. He seemed a little excited. She calmed him down and fetched his cereal. He looked kindly towards the horizon. She pulled a chair up next to him and sat down. She ground his tablets one by one and then stirred the powder into his cereal. Slowly, she gave him one spoonful at a time.

"You seem hungry," she laughed at him. Because, in her opinion, he was chewing too quickly.

Not that he's going to choke, she thought.

She gave him tea from his drink bottle. They sat next to each other and looked out to sea together. Melanie was looking at him very closely now. He didn't seem to notice how she was looking him up and down.

She could understand why her mother had fallen in love with him. He looked interesting. Her brother looked a lot like him. Unlike usual, she didn't feel anger, but pity. The beach in front of them was filling up by the hour with tourists who kept asking her if the restaurant was open.

"Unfortunately, closed today due to a death," she told anyone who asked.

It was getting pretty windy outside; even the palm trees were swaying violently back and forth, and the tourists were disappearing. It must be the storm that was raging south over the Pacific. When it was finally too windy outside, she pushed him back into the restaurant. She looked at the pictures hanging on the walls.

She suddenly turned pale and couldn't believe her eyes. She knew this picture. A recent family photo of her siblings and parents hung above the restaurant's front door. *The pictures on the ceiling and now the family photo.* She pointed to the picture hanging above the door. Kāne followed her finger, saw the picture, and out of nowhere, tears ran down his face.

No, what had she done? She didn't want that. She walked up to him, squatted down in front of him, and smiled at him.

He lifted his head and moved his mouth. She heard him softly mumble, "Ohana, family."

That hit Melanie right in the heart. She felt a pain in her chest. She stood up, pushed him into the restaurant kitchen, and read to him from the book she had discovered on the shelf in his room, "For we are only guests on Péle's land."

It was getting even stormier outside. She closed the book, heated up his vegetable porridge, stirred in his tablets, and fed him the food spoon by spoon. *He is taking enough medication to keep him alive for another 20 years,* she thought. *What kind of life is that?*

After he had eaten, she mobilised him back into bed and freshened him up again. When she had pulled his blanket up to his neck, he closed his eyes and fell asleep.

She quietly closed the door and sat down in the restaurant. It was darker outside than usual. She could hear crashing and crunching sounds everywhere. But she was immersed in old memories, so she didn't notice what was happening outside. She kept staring at the family picture. She was just six years old in it. She remembered the day it was taken. Her hair was still straight and not yet so thick and curly. She had just lost her first baby tooth that day. Her mother was young and wore her curly hair down. Her brother smiled so much that his eyes were barely recognisable. Her sister was still a toddler. Kāne wore a white shirt with jeans, just like Melanie remembered. 32 years had passed since then. What had he done? Had he changed? She knew that her mother had given him a one-way ticket and that he had never contacted them again. She lay down on an old green couch outside his room and fell fast asleep due to the lack of sleep.

A loud bang suddenly woke her up. What was that? She ran out onto Front Street and saw that the gas station and surrounding houses were on fire. This could only be another nightmare, and she wished she could wake up. But the fire was spreading rapidly. Glowing pieces of wood whirled around in the air, and the roof of the restaurant had already caught fire.

We have to get out of here, was her only thought.

Clouds of smoke formed in the house. She tore the comforter from Kāne's body, fetched the hoist, and noticed the heat from above. The flames were raging, and she was about to hook the six loops of the sling when he began to shake his head violently.

"What do you mean? You don't want to?"

He shook his head again. He winked at the door. It was getting hotter and hotter, and she had to press her shirt over her mouth. Suddenly, someone grabbed her by the arm. It was Dirk.

"Come on, we have to get out of here."

"But Kāne!"

"We won't make it. If you don't come now, you'll never see your girls again!" he shouted at her.

Melanie looked into his face in dismay. But she quickly understood: there was no other option, the flames and smoke were already everywhere. She hugged her father tightly, stroked his head, and said to him: "*Ekala mai'ia'u"*—(I'm sorry). Then she and Dirk walked out across Front Street towards the beach.

"Where are the children?" she shouted at Dirk.

"They are in the sea. It's the only safe place for them. It would be far too dangerous for them here; everything is on fire."

They ran across the sand into the sea to their children. They took all four girls in their arms.

"What about Kāne?" the twin sisters shouted.

"We didn't manage to get him out in time."

The twin sisters began to cry so loudly that Melanie's heart was almost torn apart.

She shouted, "It all happened so quickly, I couldn't save him!"

They watched as the surrounding houses and the restaurant completely collapsed.

"It looks like a war zone," muttered Leilani.

They heard cars honking and shouting.

Melanie shouted, "Turn around and look at the waves!"

Dirk took Melanie in his arms. "I thought I was losing you."

Then she started to cry. Her eyes were burning, and she couldn't breathe.

"I will never be able to forget the sight of my father." He had asked them to leave him there to let him die. "How are we going to get home?" Melanie looked at her husband sadly with her ashen face.

"The car is about 1.5 kilometres away. The girls and I ran along the beach as fast as we could. Go, here are the car keys."

"No, you're coming with me."

"Honey, I have to help. People need help. I have to help, darling. Please understand."

Melanie saw his expression; nothing could have changed his mind. "I'll call you. Your cell phone is in the car."

Dirk gave everyone a kiss and walked towards Front Street.

Melanie ran with the children in the opposite direction to the area not affected by the flames as fast as they could. They got into the car, and their cell phone showed a few missed calls. Kanaloa had tried several times. With trembling hands, she dialed him, but Haumea answered.

"Melanie, are you all right?" she asked.

"We're fine, the girls, Dirk is helping the people. But we couldn't save Kāne."

It was only then that Melanie realised what she had just told her grandmother. For a few seconds, it was quiet on the other side of the line. Melanie was crying again, her tears rolling inexorably down her cheeks.

"I'm sorry, it all happened so quickly," she cried through the receiver.

Koa picked up the phone, "But the children are all right?" she heard him call anxiously into the receiver.

"Yes, they're in the car with me. Dirk is trying to help. I can't explain where the fire came from. So quickly. We weren't warned," Melanie sobbed through the receiver. Your house is on fire, and all the surrounding houses, too, Koa."

Koa fell silent for a few seconds. "The main thing is that you're all right."

"Koa, I wanted to save him, but—"

He interrupted her, "Melanie, it's not your fault. We'll talk later when we've landed. Take the children home. I'm sure Dirk will be fine."

When she had hung up, she called Dirk, but he didn't answer her call. She had to be strong because the children were already suffering far too much. She slowly drove back to Wailuku. She looked through the rear-view mirror into the girls' crying eyes. Leilani was sitting next to her, and Melanie squeezed her hand tightly.

She turned on the radio and listened to the news.

"A large fire, ignited by the strong winds, passes through Lahaina."

Helicopters with water gallons flew in the air.

Helicopters with reporters reporting live from them.

"There is hardly anything left of the city. 2700 houses are in flames. For the residents, the flames came out of nowhere. They fled in cars, on foot, or jumped into the ocean in distress. The authorities reported that they, too, had been taken by surprise. The power failure and destroyed cell phone towers made communication difficult. Several small fires turned into one large one," the reporters reported.

They spoke of 50 deaths already.

Stunned, she drove on slowly. Dozens of fire engines, ambulances, and US Army vehicles raced towards them with blue lights flashing.

It was just 6:30 p.m. when they arrived home. She tried to reach Dirk again, but once again, he didn't answer. They turned on the news and now saw the extent of the disaster.

"The deadliest forest fire in American history," they said. *"Buildings are still collapsing. Strong winds*

helped the fire spread quickly. Weather data shows that a category 4 tropical cyclone passed to the south of Hawaii. The hurricane caused winds to reach up to 100 kilometres per hour on the island of Maui. This strong wind drove the fire further and further west towards the coastal town of Lahaina. Burning grass and other objects were carried away and started new fires," the newscasters said.

"The special geographical location of Lahaina also plays a role. The small town lies at the foot of a mountain range that slopes steeply down to the coast. The gusts of wind from the hurricane blew over this chain and then crashed down again on the downwind side. They were channelled through the deep canyons directly to Lahaina. The fire was fuelled by months of drought. Strong gusts of wind made the extinguishing work more difficult," they reported.

"The hospitals are overcrowded. They do not have enough staff to help the fire victims and smoke-intoxicated people as quickly as possible. 14,000 people are currently being taken off the island, and another 14,500 are still to be evacuated."

The governor addressed the entire state in a press conference, "If you have room at home, if you can accommodate someone from West Maui, please do so. The community centre has been converted into an emergency shelter. But there is not room for everyone. Hundreds of people are homeless."

Melanie switched off the television.

"Kids, I'm going out to sea."

They jumped up and followed Melanie into the garage. They all grabbed a surfboard and paddled out to sea in their clothes. They sat side by side in the lineup and watched as the black clouds of smoke from Lahaina rose high into the sky. They folded their hands and prayed.

Later, in the shower, Melanie kept seeing the sick man lying in front of her, begging her to let him lie down. She cried the pain out of her soul. She made up her eyes as best she could because she didn't want the girls to see her like that.

Then, she finally received a message from Dirk telling her that he was fine. And that he would be home later with Kaleo. Relieved by his message, she pulled herself together and made the girls some spaghetti. They sat together in the living room and looked towards Lahaina, where dark clouds of smoke continued to rise into the sky.

At 9.30 p.m., the doorbell rang. The children were asleep. Kehaulani and Haumea were standing in front of the door.

"Haumea, what are you doing here?" Melanie looked at her sadly.

"I wanted to see you." She entered and gave Melanie a long hug.

They sat down in the living room, and Melanie told them what had happened.

"We're lucky you're all right. Luckily, the children weren't there," said Kehaulani.

"I wanted to save him, Haumea. I really did. But the fire came so quickly. Shortly after we were in the sea, your house collapsed in the flames."

Kehaulani began to cry. "Poor Kāne. Now we have no home. What are we supposed to live on? Maui is one of the most famous vacation destinations in America. Everything depends on tourism. What should we do now?"

Haumea put her hand on her thigh, "We'll manage; we just have to stick together. You have the papaya plantation."

Kehaulani sobbed, "Thank God our children are safe and sound."

She crept up to her girls and lay down with them.

"He begged me to leave him there, Haumea. But I would have taken him out if the flames hadn't been so fast."

"I know, Melanie."

Tears rolled down Haumea's cheeks. "You shouldn't watch your children die, but he was seriously ill," she cried quietly.

They heard a car pull up and ran out. It was Dirk and Kaleo.

"Where are Lono and Koa?" asked Haumea anxiously.

They both looked at the ground and said they would help the rescue workers. They were covered from top to bottom in black soot. In the living room, they told the women that they had seen countless corpses in cars, on the street, and in houses.

"They were badly injured," reported Dirk. "I'm not sure if some of them will make it." He looked at Melanie with teary eyes as he said, "I have seen kids..."

He didn't speak any further. Melanie had never seen him cry before. She hugged him, but unlike usual, she found no words of comfort.

She prepared a bed for Haumea in the dressing room. Kaleo drove home first. He wanted to have a short rest and drive back to Lahaina with Dirk at 5 a.m.

Melanie kept seeing this man lying in the flames during the night. She couldn't fall asleep. When Dirk got up, she gave him a kiss and said, "Take care of yourself."

But she couldn't sleep any longer and quietly went into the kitchen shortly after him. Haumea and Kehaulani were already waiting sleepily in the kitchen.

The silence was so oppressive. Melanie switched on the news.

"Meanwhile, 74 bodies have been recovered," news reports said. *"According to a statement, the island state of Hawaii has the largest outdoor alarm system in the world. Around 400 sirens, 80 of them on Maui.*

Authorities have been criticised for not sounding siren alarms. The Coast Guard rescued people from the sea. The US government is supporting the local authorities with helicopters and money," it was reported.

Melanie was horrified, so many corpses.

"*Many bodies are unrecognisable. There is no official announcement about the number of missing persons. The authorities have asked the relatives of the missing persons to provide their DNA in order to facilitate the identification of the victims. Refrigerated containers have arrived on the island to store the remains,*" they added.

They sat there stunned. By now, the girls were already in the living room.

Kehaulani reassured her girls that their father and grandfather were still not there. However, Koa had sent her a message every hour to say that they were well.

"Of course you can stay with us for as long as you like, Kehaulani."

"That's very nice. We will gladly accept your offer for the time being."

"If you need money, I can help you," Haumea added.

Kehaulani hugged them both gratefully.

"That's what family is for," said Haumea. "Melanie, I think it's time you told the whole family."

Melanie was in tears.

Melanie looked at Haumea and said, "I can't tell them. Please, you tell them."

She nodded in agreement, folded her hands on her thighs, and turned her face towards Kehaulani and her twin girls. "Your uncle, the sick man who died in the fire yesterday, was Melanie's father."

The twin sisters and Kehaulani looked terrified.

"That means you are the daughter. You are one of his three children," said Kehaulani.

Melanie said, "I'm sorry. I didn't mean to trick you. The whole thing is complicated."

Kiana said, "Then, Haumea is your great-grandmother," and looked at Leilani and Lanea enthusiastically.

Haumea sobbed. "That I can still experience this. Thank you, Melanie, for coming from so far away. I searched for you for a long time. But there were no traces of you. At least not under your surname."

Melanie nodded. Her mother's new husband had adopted her, and they had taken her stepfather's surname relatively quickly.

Kiana and Kalea beamed as they quickly realised that they were also related.

"What a sad story, Melanie," Kehaulani added. "Now you've found your father, and then he dies in your hands."

Melanie shook her head. "Please don't take this the wrong way. But I didn't see him as my father. After such a long time without contact, he was more of a stranger than my father. I'm sorry he was ill."

"Welcome to the family," said Haumea.

The doorbell rang. It was Lono and Koa. They both looked ten years older. Their clothes and faces were black with soot. They hardly spoke, and Melanie gave them fresh clothes.

When they were both showered, sitting in the living room and somewhat responsive, Haumea said to them, "It's very bad what Lahaina and you are going through. My son died, but we all know that it was a redemption for him. What God has given us in return is his daughter, Melanie."

They both looked over at Melanie, puzzled.

"Yes, it's true," she stammered, "I'm sorry I didn't tell you. It's complicated."

"I recognised her at first sight," Haumea added.

"When you told me that a half-Hawaiian from Germany called Melanie was looking after your children, I had to have a look at her. And at the surfing competition, I was sure it could only be her."

Wordlessly, they approached Melanie and said, "Our heartfelt condolences. It's good that you're here."

Melanie was still ashamed because she had fooled them. But it seemed to have been forgiven and forgotten.

"Come on, kids, let's get breakfast ready," said Kehaulani and left. Suddenly, they heard the shattering of glass. When everyone rushed into the kitchen, Kehaulani was standing among the shards, in tears.

"My father is dead! My mother couldn't save him," and she fell to the floor.

Lono and Koa grabbed her by the arms and carried her into the living room.

"How terrible," said Haumea. "The family must stick together."

When Kehaulani had calmed down a little, Melanie tended to her wounds.

"I know it's not the right time, but we need to make preparations. We have to organise the burial of Kāne."

"I'll take care of that, if I may?" Melanie asked the group. "A water funeral here on the beach, if you don't mind."

The rest of the family agreed.

THE LEGACY

"Koa, you need new accommodation and work for your family," Haumea said to him.

"The Kona plantation on Big Island belonged to Kāne. So the inheritance goes to his children."

Koa, Lono, and Melanie's eyes widened.

"I don't want his inheritance," she said quickly. "It's not mine receive. Give it to Koa, please. You have nothing left."

"I'm afraid, Melanie, it's not that simple. Each of them has their own plantation, and Koa inherits the papaya plantation from his father, Lono. Koa will be able to make a good living from it if he gets involved. The plantation is in the north of Maui."

Melanie had an idea and said to him, "We have enough space here for another cottage. It would be wonderful if you could set up your new home here. I'm sure Dirk wouldn't mind."

Koa looked at her and fell silent. Kehaulani tearfully thanked her for the offer.

"We should talk to Kanaloa. He's been taking care of the Kona plantation on Big Island since his brother got sick," Koa said.

They sent Kanaloa a message to come to Maui as soon as possible. Lono and Koa went to sleep in the girls' rooms upstairs. The rest of the family went outside towards the surf school. The girls played soccer. They waited for Dirk and Koa to come back. At lunchtime, they saw the men walking towards them. Melanie ran towards them.

They were also black from top to bottom from all the ash. The family sat at the beach bar, and they told them about the suffering but also about the rescues. A short time later, Kanaloa, Lono, and Koa joined them. Koa and Lono had already told Kanaloa that Melanie was Kāne's daughter. He met her with heartfelt condolences and greeted her with a big hug. Together, they planned the funeral and the construction of the new house on her property. They postponed the plantation meeting until after the funeral.

"Did you find his body?" Haumea asked anxiously.

Dirk and Kaleo looked very sad. "The helpers found his body with sniffer dogs and recovered it. But they still want a DNA sample," and they looked at Melanie.

"Of course, I'll do that. I'm going to the community center first thing tomorrow."

"Is it even necessary?" Haumea asked the group.

"He's not missing. We just need to tell the Forensic anthropologists that Kāne was the only one in your house who died."

"No, unfortunately, that's not possible, Mom. It could be someone else. They want security," said Kanaloa.

They prayed together for the victims, the injured and their families.

In the evening, Haumea and Kanaloa flew back to Kauai. Kehaulani drove with Koa to her mother. Now Melanie had time to catch up with her siblings. They met via group chat. They were shocked at how ill he had been. She told them about the pictures. They were sad to hear about his death. But to them, he was also just a stranger. They wanted to take leave for the funeral. Melanie and Dirk cleared the rooms on the upper floor for the Binkom family. Leilani and Lanea were given the dressing room in the basement. This gave each family a temporary retreat.

When the children were asleep, the parents sat together in the living room.

While they were watching the news, it was announced that the town of Lahaina was inaccessible to tourists for the time being. But the residents would be allowed to rescue their belongings. They warned of toxic substances that had collected in the ground. And because of this, the water in large parts of the city was too contaminated to drink. Maui Humane Society staff worked tirelessly to help the disoriented, frightened, and injured animals.

Five days later, Melanie received a letter from the DNA testing center. She opened the letter, which read:

DNA Test Report: Mr Kāne Binkom possesses the hereditary characteristics required for the father of the child, Melanie Muleiula Stein, in all DNA systems examined. He is, therefore, a possible father. This resulted in a paternity probability of 99.9999 %. Based on the available test results and the biostatic evaluation, it is practically proven that Mr Kāne Binkom is the biological father of the child, Melanie Muleiula Stein.

She immediately told the family. Because they were sure that it was his body, they could now bury him.

Five days later, the closest family members met on the private beach in front of their house. It was Leilani's birthday.

The families gathered in front of their house on the beach. Dirk helped Haumea and Ku into the canoe. The rest of the family had their surfboards ready. As Melanie, her brother, and sister carefully placed the urn on their favourite surfboard, she and the girls carefully swam out to sea with it. They stopped line-up, and the rest gathered around them on their surfboards. Each of them wore a colourful flower lei around their necks. The entire line-up said goodbye to Kāne as Melanie spread the ashes over the shiny blue water, and the rest placed their flower leis on the water's surface. After the wreaths of flowers were slowly carried off into the distance by the waves, everyone paddled back to the beach together.

Gathered on the porch, Leilani unpacked her presents.

Meanwhile, Ku quietly took Melanie aside on the beach steps.

In the background, she heard Leilani shout: "An e-foilsurf board!"

Melanie smiled gratefully at Haumea.

"I want you to take over the inheritance," Ku said to her.

"To be honest, we don't have the tourists. We hardly rent out any surfboards. And it will be a while before people want to come to the island again."

"So you're taking it? It's all yours."

"The Kona plantation on the Big Island?" she asked her great-grandfather, her eyes shining.

Ku smiled. "Yes, the Kona plantation on the Big Island."

"Why did he inherit the biggest one of all?"

"Because he was my first child. The Kona plantation was the first in our family."

Melanie paused for a moment, and Ku looked at her worriedly. She remembered the nightmare when she was holding a coffee bean and a volcano had erupted. But Melanie looked Ku resolutely in the face, and said,

"Then I'll carry on the family estate." She hugged her Grandfather Ku tentatively.

Once they had sorted that out, they saw Leilani happily surfing along the water on her e-foil surfboard.

ABOUT THE AUTHOR

Melanie Michelle Rosenthal, née Phipps, was born in 1984 in el Paso, Texas. She is a trained industrial clerk. She lives in Germany with her daughters and her husband. She and her husband are both entrepreneurs. She is half-Hawaiian, lives the aloha spirit, and lives by the sea. In her book, she writes about the beautiful islands of Hawaii, her culture, and her great passion for surfing.

www.ingramcontent.com/pod-product-compliance
Lightning Source LLC
Chambersburg PA
CBHW050244010526
44107CB00003B/179